PLAYING THE UNCONSCIOUS

PSYCHOANALYTIC INTERVIEWS WITH CHILDREN USING WINNICOTT'S SQUIGGLE TECHNIQUE

Michael Günter

KARNAC

First published in 2007 by
Karnac Books Ltd
118 Finchley Road
London NW3 5HT

British Library Cataloguing in Publication Data

A C.I.P for this book is available from the British Library

ISBN-13: 978–1–85575–419–5

Translated by Harriet Hasenclever

Edited, designed, and produced by
Florence Production Ltd, Stoodleigh, Devon
www.florenceproduction.co.uk

Printed in Great Britain
www.karnacbooks.com

For Franziska, Daphne and Florentine

CONTENTS

ACKNOWLEDGEMENTS

First of all my thanks go to the children and young people who placed such hopes in our interviews that they were willing to allow me a glimpse of the vulnerable side of their inner lives. I learn from them constantly and continue to be astonished at the variety that meets me in these encounters. My thanks are also greatly due to my family, my three wonderful daughters and my wife, for their patience with me over this project when I was more absent than usual. Above all I thank them for reminding me that there is such a thing as a real life outside work.

I should like to thank my colleagues at the clinic, above all Gunther Klosinski, for their very considerate attitude on days when I was more occupied with squiggles than with other things. I am grateful to them all for clinical discussions and valuable suggestions. Working with Dr Beyer of my German publishers Klett-Cotta was both enjoyable and helpful in making the publication of this book possible. For the illustrations, Christel Beck of Klett-Cotta managed to conjure the optimum from the original, often indistinct drawings. There were passages in the German original which my translator, Harriet Hasenclever, discussed with me at length until we had teased out exactly what was meant, so that the translated version feels close to my text and to my way of thinking. Finally I wish to thank Christelle Yeyet-Jacquot and Oliver Rathbone of Karnac for the supportive way in which, despite a number of difficulties, they have accompanied the implementation of this project of creating an English edition.

ABOUT THE AUTHOR

Michael Günter
Priv. Doz. Dr med. Michael Günter is senior lecturer and senior head physician in the Department of Psychiatry and Psychotherapy for Children and Adolescents at the University of Tübingen. He is a child and adolescent psychiatrist and psychoanalyst (DPV/IPS) and also a medical specialist in psychotherapeutic medicine. In addition, he edits the journal *Kinderanalyse*.

Brett Kahr
Senior Clinical Research Fellow in Psychotherapy and Mental Health at the Centre for Child Mental Health in London, and Winnicott Clinic Senior Research Fellow in Psychotherapy at the Winnicott Clinic of Psychotherapy, and Patron of the Squiggle Foundation. Author of *D.W. Winnicott: A Biographical Portrait*, and editor of *Forensic Psychotherapy and Psychopathology: Winnicottian Perspectives* and *The Legacy of Winnicott: Essays on Infant and Child Mental Health.*

FOREWORD
Brett Kahr

When the young twenty-something Dr Donald Winnicott accepted a post as Assistant Physician at the Paddington Green Children's Hospital in West London in 1923, he found himself confronted with a dilemma. Although employed as an ordinary physician in children's medicine—the term "paediatrician" not yet having come into vogue—engaged to practice standard British medicine, the maverick Winnicott had already begun to take a strong interest in Freudian psychoanalysis, and he would soon embark upon a six-day weekly analysis with Freud's principal English language translator, Mr James Strachey. Winnicott's analysis gradually took root, and by 1927 he had enrolled as one of the very first trainees at the Institute of Psycho-Analysis in London, ultimately qualifying in both adult psychoanalysis and child psychoanalysis. This exposure to the early Freudians changed Winnicott's fledgling paediatric work from a study of children's temperatures and fevers to an examination of the hidden unconscious processes and private psychological torments in youngsters and their parents.

Winnicott had to endure much suspicion and hostility from his senior medical colleagues at Paddington Green Children's Hospital, many of whom thought him rather odd, to say the least; and no doubt through his considerable personal charm, he managed to survive execution, and retained his post for fully forty years. Eventually, however, he began to specialise in psychologically orientated cases, leaving much of the physical medicine to his registrars and to his other senior colleagues. By the 1940s, he had developed his so-called

"Psychiatric Snack Bar" at Paddington Green, a place where parents could bring their children for a single assessment, a place where Winnicott could experiment with his so-called "therapeutic consultations", attempting to use infant observation and play therapy in an effort to uncover the family secrets or unconscious conflicts which might have contributed to a psychosomatic symptom in the child.

Not only did Winnicott enter medicine at a time when colleagues denigrated the fledgling field of paediatrics—a low-status profession compared with surgery, for instance—but he did so at a time when Great Britain boasted few psychiatrists, and even fewer *child* psychiatrists. Indeed, the first British textbook on child psychiatry did not appear until 1939 with the publication of Dr Ronald Gordon's edited text on *A Survey of Child Psychiatry*, to which Winnicott himself contributed a chapter on "The Psychology of Juvenile Rheumatism". As a pioneer of British child psychiatry, Winnicott faced a further dilemma: as a very scant resource, how could he possibly provide treatment for the many thousands and thousands of young babies, toddlers, latency-age children, and adolescents who attended his Psychiatric Snack Bar? With few child psychiatrists available, and almost none with intensive psychotherapeutic or psychoanalytic training, Winnicott knew that he would have to cut corners, as he certainly could not provide in-depth, five times weekly child analysis for each of these arrivals, nor would such intensive treatment be needed in most cases.

From this problematic situation, Winnicott cleverly developed the squiggle game as a rapid means of making safe contact with troubled children—a method which combined Winnicott's love of playfulness with his love of psychoanalysis, and with his love of painting and drawing. As Winnicott's first biographer, I have on many occasions consulted the two principal depositories of Winnicott's personal and professional papers now housed partly in New York City and partly in London, and I can report that Winnicott loved to scrawl on many of his professional letters, some of which he literally smothered in squiggles and doodles, penned in his characteristically swirly handwriting. Winnicott also sent hand-painted Christmas cards to his nearest and dearest every year, and though this proved a time-consuming late-night activity, Winnicott took great pleasure in producing his Christmas cards. Thus it seemed only natural that a man with such a need for artistic expression would endeavour to find a way to bring this love affair with the arts into his consulting room.

The squiggle game permitted Winnicott to process a large number of cases with reasonable speed, establishing immediate therapeutic contact, melting through the defences, and arriving at the buried conflict beneath the symptom. One must hasten to add, however, that although Donald Winnicott made the squiggle game look "easy"—rather like Fred Astaire's dancing—he often stated that he needed his entire multi-year training in child psychoanalysis just to facilitate one short squiggle game. Only a master practitioner of in-depth analysis could dare to produce a shortened version and still manage to "hold" the complexity of the operation.

In similar fashion, Professor Dr med. Michael Günter has utilised his comprehensive training in general medicine, with further specialisation in paediatrics and child psychiatry, and in adult and child psychoanalysis—exactly the training that Winnicott had undertaken—to develop the squiggle game further as a solid, sober, effective, and above all, compassionate technique for making contact with troubled children and teenagers in his hospital and clinic consultative work. An artist himself by background, who has written extensively on the use of art as a treatment tool in the psychiatric hospital, Professor Günter seems ideally placed to develop this "art form" of the squiggle game in the practice of child psychiatry. Deeply experienced in working with children suffering from crippling and fatal diseases, Günter has pioneered the use of the psychoanalytically orientated squiggle game not only in the psychiatric hospital, but in the general medical setting as well.

Though deeply indebted to the work of Winnicott, Professor Günter does not idealise him in an uncritical manner; in fact, he has sagely observed that before Winnicott started to write about the squiggle game, the legendary Viennese psychoanalyst and art historian, Dr Ernst Kris, had already made a pioneering contribution to the field through his study of the psychology of doodling. As Winnicott knew both Dr Ernst Kris and his wife Dr Marianne Kris, herself the daughter of Freud's card-partner Dr Oskar Rie, it may well be, as Günter politely suggests, that Winnicott's interest in the squiggle technique may have received some early encouragement from contact with Kris, an interesting historical speculation that deserves further consideration, especially in view of the fact that after their flight from Vienna, the Krises lived in London for a short period of time before settling, finally, in New York City.

As soon as one begins to read Günter's writing, one begins to like him immediately. Not only does he write with exceptional clarity and with great economy, he also transmits an attitude of deep concern and compassion for his patients, which can only be described as admirable. He shares his concerns about confidentiality with his young patients and reflects upon his desire to protect their privacy; he also shares his personal anxieties about the risk of exposing his own unconscious processes to the child through *his* contributions to the squiggle game; and he succeeds in communicating his highly-honed capacity to be both serious and playful at the same time, never losing sight of his psychotherapeutic task, but never frightening the child with awkward, intrusive questions or caricatured psycho-analytical interpretations which might in fact have an iatrogenic quality. Günter talks with his patients in a conversational style, imbued, however, with his encyclopaedic psychoanalytical and psychiatric knowledge and his decades of dedicated clinical experience. After reading Günter's cases, one feels pleased on behalf of the child patients that each has managed to find such a sensitive and creative healer. One also feels hopeful for the future of psychoanalysis and psychotherapy to have found such a trustworthy and sturdy guide into the world of the child's pain and suffering.

Although Winnicott's work on the squiggle game has received international recognition, we must not avoid the fact that Winnicott never developed a training school; therefore, one still cannot become officially qualified as a "Winnicottian child psychotherapist". In Great Britain, the vast majority of child psychotherapists will be steeped principally in the Kleinian and post-Kleinian traditions, with a smaller percentage soaked in the writings of Anna Freud. Pioneering British child psychotherapists Ann Horne and Monica Lanyado have recently begun to edit a series of books on Independent Tradition thinking in child psychotherapy, deeply influenced by Winnicottianism, and this will correct the balance considerably. As for the squiggle game, although most child psychotherapists do use play therapy techniques, I know of virtually none who actually use the squiggle game in the systematic manner of Winnicott and Günter, and this seems a lost opportunity. London-based child psychiatrist and child psychoanalyst Dr Abrahão Brafman remains a noted exception, and in his own work on squiggles, the brilliantly crafted *Untying the Knot: Working with Children and Parents*, he has kept Winnicott's tradition alive, and he has even extended it in his own characteristically wise fashion.

The practice of the squiggle game requires a great deal of courage from a number of perspectives. First of all, most child psychologists and child psychotherapists use verbal exchange as their primary mode of relatedness. Those who do introduce play therapy measures into their work tend to remain neutral, allowing the patient to draw or to use a sand tray, while themselves observing and interpreting from the sidelines, anxious not to intrude upon the child's experience of play. Therefore, the active participation of the clinician in the squiggle game could hardly be described as standard technique. And yet in the hands of a Winnicott, or a Brafman, or a Günter, the squiggle game becomes the ultimate expression of *relationality*, and if deployed safely, as Günter always does, it can provide the child with a unique forum in which to communicate.

Winnicott himself used the squiggle game during his visits to Finland, and although he spoke virtually no Finnish, he impressed at least one little boy who remembered him as the man who spoke *excellent* Finnish. Perhaps the squiggle game may come to represent a more preverbal, universal language that can cut through educational differences, class differences, racial differences, sexual differences, intelligence differences and the like, and provide the child with a wonderful means of engaging in contact with the psychotherapist or doctor who may be perceived at first as quite a scary figure.

Michael Günter's book brings his clinical work to life in a joyful, vivid manner, and it pleases me to know that his professional contributions, long admired by German-speaking colleagues and students, will now become available to the English-speaking audience. I regard Professor Günter's work as an outstanding achievement in the art and science of psychotherapy, and also in Winnicott studies, and I feel confident that his book will soon become a talking point in the child mental health community in Great Britain and beyond, and hopefully in the adult mental health community as well. I congratulate Professor Günter on his warm-hearted clinical accomplishment, and I await his further contributions in this field and in related ones with great interest and anticipation.

CHAPTER ONE

Introduction: practice and theory of the squiggle game

The idea of writing a book on the Winnicott squiggle game in therapeutic work with children has been in my mind for a long time and is rooted in many experiences. One such is the realisation, still surprising to me even after so many years, that the squiggle game does indeed enable us in most cases to make contact with a child with particular ease. In most cases, if the child takes up my suggestion, an intense dialogue develops in one way or another, which gives an insight into his or her inner situation. And even in cases where the child is consciously very reserved and in which the talk emerging from the squiggle game seems to be unproductive, the pictures offer a chance to start talking about precisely why he or she shows such reserve.

Naturally, squiggles are not a magical all-purpose psycho-therapeutic tool. There are cases in which I don't know much more about the child and his or her conflicts and subjective view of things after our conversation than I had already been told by the parents. It would also be a mistake to suppose that the ease with which children make contact through squiggles is carried over into virtually effortless diagnostic and therapeutic work. It is important to set up the psychotherapeutic interview situation to be playful in character, which is incidentally fun for both therapist and child. The squiggle game makes this easier because it generates a playful atmosphere, which nevertheless has a very serious side. Results emerge from a genuinely therapeutic form of work; however, this can be extremely taxing. I am sometimes even tempted to avoid an encounter as

1

intense as the squiggle game produces, and simply have a friendly conversation with the child.

Lest there be any misunderstanding, let me point out right at the start that these case studies describe the events as they happened. Most of them I have given in full; only in one or two cases have I abridged the account because the material was so voluminous. The same goes for the pictures: with very few exceptions, I have included the whole sequence, that is to say those I made out of the children's squiggles as well as those which I consider far more important: the pictures the children made out of mine. It was possible to reconstruct the interviews in such detail either because I made notes on the pages we were using for the squiggles and then wrote them up in detail straight after the session, or because a younger colleague sat in on the sessions and noted everything practically verbatim. Nevertheless, the case studies offered here and the associated insights into clinical practice, technical points of treatment and theory are naturally the result of a process of reflection which occurred when I revisited them whilst preparing the material for publication. This also means that some of the interpretations that seem so obvious after the event did not cross my mind at all during the interview. It is surprising how blind one can be during the session. The way things went was often determined not so much by conscious insight on my part as by intuition and by the fact that I had a theory of the emotional development of the child "in my bones", as Winnicott aptly termed the basis of this work. In psychoanalytical terms, this form of intuition is communication from unconscious to unconscious, and it is precisely this form of communication that joins conscious communication in the squiggle interviews and makes them so fascinating and therapeutically effective.

Some of the insights took on a clear form in the course of the interview, and I offered the child my interpretation. Some first crystallized after our conversation, although on re-reading it is clear that they played a significant role in our communication. Yet others only began to stand out clearly enough for me to feel I had really grasped them while I was working through the material. We should not be daunted by the mass of material and layers of possible meanings that are presented. In the session itself we should hold back and be sparing with interpretations. These often do not help the child to feel understood and are sometimes more likely to inhibit the flow of communication. It is possible that some of these interpretations may be more helpful to the therapist, giving him a firm footing from which he can focus and structure a confusing mass of material. Even this is legitimate, but it should not be confused with allowing the child to reach an insight and feel understood. Nevertheless, interpretations which address an identifiable conflict in the child are sometimes very important, and I am convinced that they have a therapeutic effect if the child feels emotionally understood. The squiggle game does not differ here from other techniques of psycho-analytically oriented psychotherapy which also assume that intellectual insight alone cannot have any effect. I find it impossible to define exactly when I would consider interpretations appropriate and when they should be avoided if at all possible. It is my belief that in the end it is a question of clinical experience and of assessing the whole clinical situation.

In his book on squiggle interviews, Winnicott (1971a) stressed how important it is to be ready to withdraw our comments at all times if a child reacts to an interpretation with rejection or apparently doesn't react at all. He felt it was important to allow the child a chance to correct the therapist. Even an interpretation which is correct in itself will not be taken in by the child if it is given at the wrong moment or in the wrong way. A dogmatic interpretation will in his opinion allow the child only two possible options: to accept what has been said as propaganda, or to reject the interpretation, the therapist and the whole set-up. In this respect it is important in these conversations to let ourselves be led by the child, and I often let two or three pictures go by, waiting until I am really sure that the child wishes to enter into a relationship with me, rather than give an interpretation too early, as this might trigger subservience or withdrawal.

In mentioning Winnicott I have already named the author of my second and obviously most decisive inspiration to write this book, which I have long had in mind. It is his incomparable book *Therapeutic Consultations in Child Psychiatry* on the use of psycho-analysis in child psychiatry, published in England in 1971 and reprinted in 1996. In this book and in a few other publications on the subject, Winnicott refers to his technique as the squiggle game. His general characterization of what psychotherapy is, formulated in his book *Playing and Reality* (1971b), could also serve as a *leitmotif* for this book:

Psychotherapy takes place in the overlap of two areas of playing: that of the patient and that of the therapist. Psychotherapy has to do with two people playing together. The corollary of this is that where playing is not possible then the work done by the therapist is directed towards bringing the patient from a state of not being able to play into a state of being able to play. [p. 38]

The stress on playfulness is a thread running through the whole of *Therapeutic Consultations in Child Psychiatry*, which consists in essence of twenty case studies interwoven with Winnicott's commentaries. Winnicott pays great attention in the squiggle game, as in his other psychoanalytical work, to offering a space within which the potential for play in the child's psyche can unfold. In his essay "The Squiggle Game" (1968), he writes: "The principle is that psychotherapy is done in an overlap of the area of play of the child and the area of play of the adult or therapist. The squiggle game is one example of the way in which such play may be facilitated."

This is not the place to review the book in all its facets and richness of thought, but I would like to mention at least a few aspects which are important to me. The first great advantage of the book is that with the help of the squiggles and near-verbatim dialogues we can follow exactly what actually happened in the session even without being able to look at formal transcripts. The chance to gain a detailed insight into the working style of an analyst is a rarity in the psychoanalytical literature, which alone makes his work one of the most important books on psychoanalysis. It is fascinating to read, and although focused on playful communication, the text is never simply a one-to-one copy of what happened, but is informed throughout with thoughts on the dynamics and genesis of the patient's illness and problems, and complemented with comments on theory and techniques in treatment. In this way his book is a treasure trove for the child psychotherapist, child psychiatrist, educational consultant and child analyst.

After a brief introduction, Winnicott begins his description of his first case with the simple explanation of the squiggle game that he gives to his patient: "I shut my eyes and go like this on the paper and you turn it into something, and then it's your turn and you do something and I turn it into something. . ." (1971a, p. 12)—and already both are engrossed. Winnicott stresses repeatedly how important it is to create an atmosphere in which the child can feel free enough. He lets the child know, for example, that the game he wants to play has no rules. He asks the child to show him if his squiggle looks like anything in particular or if he or she can make anything out of it. Then the child will do the same for him and he will see if he can make anything out of the child's squiggle (1968). Sometimes I find it also makes sense, especially with older, slightly inhibited children who might see the whole thing in terms of performance requirements as in art classes at school, to tell them it's not a question of drawing a beautiful picture, just to allay any fears they might have.

The therapist's task is a double one: on the one hand to let himself be drawn into the game with the child, and on the other hand to provide a holding framework. This is what Winnicott means when he writes in his essay that he understands the squiggle game better than the children do. It is his task, and he knows how, to create the framework for "the child's own discovery of what was already there in herself" (1968, p. 316; cf. 1971a, p. 62). But, he adds, the children are better at drawing. They depict what it's all about. Both the unfolding of the game and the holding framework are essential parts of a successful therapeutic dialogue. In this the therapist must above all be able to "provide a natural, freely moving human relationship within the professional setting while the patient gradually surprises himself by the production of ideas and feelings that have not been previously integrated into the total personality. Perhaps the main work done is of the nature of integration, made possible by the reliance on the human but professional relationship—a form of 'holding'." (1968, p. 299) The development of the game and the freedom and involvement with which the therapist adds his contribution to the game are of critical importance in making it work. In contrast to a physical examination or a psychological test, a procedure of this kind evokes no feeling of inferiority. Winnicott emphasized on many occasions the importance of child and therapist meeting on an equal footing in game and conversation. He was also rather reluctant to describe the technique. He was worried that

someone will be likely to begin to re-write what I describe as if it were a set technique with rules and regulations. Then the whole value of the procedure would be lost. If I describe what I do there is a very real danger that others will take it and form it into something that corresponds to a Thematic Apperception Test. The difference between this and a T.A.T. is firstly that it is not a test, and secondly that the consultant contributes from his own ingenuity almost as much as the child does . . . Naturally, the consultant's contribution drops out, because it is the child, not the consultant, who is communicating distress. [1968, p. 301]

Winnicott points out that "it is necessary for the consultant to be ready to learn rather than to be eager to pounce on the material with interpretations!" (Winnicott 1968, p. 300)—and it is precisely this approach which produces such good results.

It was his intention, he wrote, to present examples for communication with children. In this respect he makes it clear that it would be wrong for someone to learn how to use the game and think that this equipped them to conduct therapy.

The squiggle game is simply one way of getting into contact with a child. What happens in the game and in the whole course of the interview depends on the use made of the child's experience, including the material that presents itself. In order to use the mutual experience one must have in one's bones a theory of the emotional development of the child and of the relationship of the child to the environmental factors. [1971a, p. 3]

However, Winnicott also built on the great advance of trust that children are able to give at these particular moments, which he would almost describe as sacred. If these moments were wasted, then the child's belief that he or she was understood would be destroyed. Children often told him that they had dreamt about him the night before a consultation. In these dreams their own ideas and expectations appeared, but so did those of their parents and of their environment. He was amused to be told that he was the very person they had dreamt about. In this way the therapist becomes the subjective object for the child and these wishes, expectations and fears are projected onto him.

The counterpart on the therapist's side is the holding environment (Winnicott, 1954), which he provides and which is a fundamental element of every psychoanalytical treatment. It is derived from the maternal holding function which is central to the early development of a child (Winnicott, 1960). At a very early level of psychical development, and expressed in different terms (Bion, 1962), this has to do with the therapist's containing function, which is derived from the mother's dreamlike empathy with her child (reverie). Through projective identification the child can project into the mother a part of his or her psyche which contains unbearable feelings and which he or she experiences as a bad inner object. These feelings undergo such changes when the child is at the "good breast" that they become bearable when the object is re-introjected (Klein, 1946, 1957).

Winnicott is convinced that the child is expressing the current problems, emotional conflicts or fields of tension which are dominating his or her life at the time. Alongside the conscious ones, preconscious and unconscious aspects of the child's personality and conflicts are also depicted. However, the material only becomes specific and highly interesting because the child begins to feel that he or she will be understood and may achieve communication at a significant level. As he shows above all in his theory of antisocial tendencies (1984), Winnicott always understands the patient's symptoms also as a desperate hope that his or her communications will be understood after all (Abram, 1996).

> The basis for this specialised work is the theory that a patient—child or adult—will bring to the first interview a certain amount of capacity to *believe* in getting help and to trust the one who offers help. What is needed from the helper is a strictly professional setting in which the patient is free to explore the exceptional opportunity that the consultation provides for communication. The patient's communication with the psychiatrist will have reference to the specific emotional tendencies which have a current form and which have roots that go back into the past or deep into the structure of the patient's personality and of his personal inner reality. [Winnicott, 1968 p. 299]

The squiggle game is often satisfying in itself, he writes:

> It is then like a "found object", for instance a stone or piece of old wood that a sculptor may find and set up as a kind of expression, without needing work. This appeals to lazy boys and

girls, and throws a light on the meaning of laziness. Any work done spoils what starts off as an idealised object. It may be felt by the artist that the paper or the canvas is too beautiful, it must not be spoiled. Potentially, it *is* a masterpiece. [*ibid.*, p. 302]

It is probably due in part to this idealized side of the experience that a deep understanding develops so quickly between therapist and child. However, this is also what makes it seem inadvisable to work with this technique for a number of hours. After a few sessions "all the problems of transference and of resistance begin to appear and the treatment must now be dealt with along ordinary psychoanalytic lines" (Winnicott 1971a, p. 10). Nevertheless, it is also this spontaneous, impulsive movement of the found object that frightens certain children because it is connected to the unorganized, mad parts of the self (Farhi, 2001). Winnicott points out that squiggles are uninhibited in that no limits are set, and some children find this lack of restraint naughty. For this reason it was up to him to ensure integration, but this should never go so far as to deny the chaos in any way. Naturally the children also show integrative moves, as can be seen in a number of examples in this book. For instance it can often be observed towards the end of a session, when I indicate that each of us is going to draw one more picture. Some children are then visibly anxious to reconstruct their defences and draw a picture that allows them to leave the chaos behind in the session.

Winnicott himself describes squiggle games with children between five and thirteen years of age. There seem to be two exceptions among his cases: Cecil (case 14) is noted as being 21 months old, but that was the first time Winnicott saw him; in fact he was eight when Winnicott played the squiggle game with him. The case of 30-year-old Ms X (case 18) is introduced with the comment that there is no fundamental difference between a conversation with a child and one with a parent except that with adults and older children the exchange of pictures serves no useful purpose. Winnicott therefore conducts the interview with this mother without recourse to drawing.

The children and adolescents described in detail in this book were between seven and sixteen years of age when I saw them. The squiggle technique can in fact be used successfully with children of five and even four, as the example of Paul later in this chapter shows. At the other end of the age spectrum, it has been my experience—

particularly with psychiatric patients who are severely ill, right up to adulthood—that the use of the squiggle game can sometimes break the ice, and there can suddenly be a lively exchange where previously the atmosphere had been marked by the patient's distinct withdrawal. I have not been able to collect any systematic experience in the use of the squiggle game with adults so far—my experience is limited to single instances—but in the meantime I am convinced that this kind of first contact can be very helpful with older teenagers and adults. The lower age limit is not absolute, but is largely determined by the fact that as a rule it makes more sense actually to play with very young children of two or three, and allow the psychical content to unfold within the framework of child's play. The squiggles made by these very young children are often repetitive, showing little variation, or the children lose interest fairly quickly and want to turn to something else.

A third source of interest in the writing of this book lies in my longstanding preoccupation with concepts of art therapy (Günter, 1989, 1990, 1993, 1995). Since the fundamental work of Anna Freud (1927) and Melanie Klein (1932) it has been beyond dispute that as a rule, psychoanalytical work with children is possible only by involving their play and what they create, since in such young children there can be very little reliance on verbal association. Freud described phantasy and children's play as a *Zwischenreich*, an intermediate realm between outer and inner reality (Freud, 1916/1917). In his Lectures he used the striking image of the Yellowstone Nature Reserve to capture this: a place which is removed from the need to earn a living and orientate oneself to reality, an enclosed space within which Nature can grow undisturbed (1911b, 1916/17). His famous example from *Beyond the Pleasure Principle* (1920g) also describes this intermediate position of child's play between inner and outer reality. His eighteen-month-old grandchild is playing the Fort-Da game with a bobbin, and learning through this game to tolerate his mother's absence. His description makes it clear how on the one hand this game translates the child's inner reality into action and processes it. The child wants his mother to return and would like to punish her for going away. These wishes are symbolized in the game of throwing the bobbin on its thread over the side of the cot till it disappears and pulling it back again straight away, a sequence accompanied by enunciations. On the other hand, the child also relates to outer reality and tries, through his own activity, to process and overcome his vulnerability caused by the real absence of his mother. The two elements are united in the game and its symbolic meaning.

It is precisely this intermediate realm between inner and outer reality that Winnicott takes up in his definition of creativity with its close connection to the transitional object. He depicts the emergence of the intermediate area of art, religion and culture as a whole as the attempt to find a solution for the problem of relating what is objectively perceived to what is subjectively imagined, the outer world to the inner world. This problem presents itself from earliest infancy onwards, and the way it is solved is decisive—in Winnicott's view—for the development of the personality and for a stable ego structure. "In infancy this intermediate area is necessary for the initiation of a relationship between the child and the world" (1971b, p. 13). He draws a line of development from "transitional phenomena to playing, and from playing to shared playing, and from this to cultural experiences" (*ibid.*, p. 51). Learning to accept reality is a task which is never completed, and relief from the pressure of having to relate inner to outer reality is "provided by an intermediate area of experience which is not challenged (arts, religion, etc) . . . this intermediate area is in direct continuity with the play area of the small child who is 'lost' in play" (*ibid.*, p. 13). I have already pointed out that Winnicott sees psychotherapy and play as closely related. He places both, like cultural experience, "in a creative potential space between the individual and the environment" (*ibid.*, p. 100). This "potential space" symbolizes oneness at the point at which separation has occurred.

It is not that creative activity is to be understood as a mere wallowing in "oceanic feeling". On the contrary, it bears the mark of reality and will therefore always be caught in the tension between inner and outer reality, oneness and separation, presence and absence, closeness and distance. Here we could, with Kris (1936, 1952), speak of "a regression in the service of the ego" (Kris, 1952, p. 177) in the creative process, and similarly in play. The ego uses the primary process, handles regression, and wilfully and temporarily withdraws cathexis from an area in order to regain dominance more firmly afterwards (*ibid.*, p. 187). Kris incidentally mentions doodling in this context.

Occasional observations of untrained normal individuals, as well as self-observations, suggest that doodling tends to occur while one is "unoccupied" or in a state of distracted attention, i.e. when the ego is fully occupied with something else. At first one is frequently aware of a certain purposive idea, an "intention to draw", which may refer to any geometrical or decorative design. In some instances, one may "intend" to reproduce some object in the environment; in others there is no such intention. In the course of doodling this intention gets lost. The drawing hand "creates" autonomously; lines or steps "suggest" subsequent ones, clinical observations suggest that doodling has a frequent if not regular dynamic function for the normal: fantasies and thoughts hidden in doodles are those of which the doodler wants to liberate himself, lest they disturb the process of concentration ... If we compare various observations—among them also analytic experiences—doodling comes extraordinarily close to "pre-conscious fantasy thinking ... from which it differs, however, in so far as only visual images are involved. The "archaic pictorial thought processes" have asserted themselves and the content of thoughts is transformed into visual material as in Silberer's description of hypnagogic phenomena. [Kris, 1952, UK edition 1953, p. 90]

These comments sound almost like an early theoretical explanation of Winnicott's squiggle game. It must remain an open question whether Winnicott drew his inspiration for the game from Kris, since the book was only published in 1952 and Winnicott had already begun to use the technique in 1948. In *Therapeutic Consultations in Child Psychiatry* he reports on Mark (case 15), whom he first saw when the boy was 12 and with whom he used the squiggle game. At the end of the chapter he mentions that Mark was 26 in 1962. On the other hand, precisely these passages quoted above also appeared in Kris' German paper "Bemerkungen zur Bildnerei der Geisteskranken" which was published in *Imago* in 1936.

For many children the offer of playing such a game together means above all that their fear of being too directly confronted with the therapist and having to meet his expectations is allayed. In this shared activity children often rapidly gain confidence in their ability to examine the therapist as much as they may feel examined by him.

The pictures become the means of getting into contact with one another without either feeling the other's glance as intrusive. Our eyes are not directly on the child but on the picture he or she has drawn, which takes away some of the threatening aspect of the glance. Children often also feel that communication through speech is too direct a way of approaching them and therefore too threatening—we only have to think of autistic or very withdrawn children. This explains why pictures can make the first steps to "conversation" so much easier. The threatening character of speech is connected among other things with the supposedly lesser ambiguity of language-based communication; in other words, with the discursive symbolism of language as compared to the "presentational" and much more ambiguous symbolism of pictures. Pictures require the explanation of language to be understood even if they affect us in a different way emotionally, whereas language seems at first sight to say unambiguously what is meant even though, as we know from our therapeutic practice, this is in fact by no means the case. It therefore seems much simpler, and much less threatening for some children, to hide behind the symbolism of the pictures and leave a lot open.

Paradoxically, it is precisely this that often leads children to open up rapidly and markedly as regards preconscious and unconscious content. To a certain extent, drawing presents the offer of a relationship and transference with regressive undertones, in that it allows the child at any time to distance him- or herself from any direct concern with inner conflicts and to project inner processes into the outer reality of the picture. We could say—in somewhat metaphoric terms—that the deep fears to which some children are exposed are to a certain degree projected into the outside world and put under a magic spell. This is the case particularly for children with a severe or life-threatening somatic illness, but also for children with severe psychological disorders, such as psychoses, severe anxiety disorders or borderline personality disorders. Their diffuse and also often extremely threatening fears can be given a form in the doodles. This makes such fears easier for the children to handle and often enables them initially to distance themselves from them. In this respect squiggles can be seen as a form of phantasising activity which can, like other phantasies, play a decisive role in defence against deep fears. We can see aspects of them, as did Loch in a different context

(2006, §21), as "progressive defence" in the sense of "ramparts" which "block" the access to memories, to the primal scenes.

Looking together at the pictures that emerge, it is then possible to have a therapeutic exchange about the dangerous character of, for instance, the animals depicted in them. This indirect approach to their fears seems to be far easier for children to tolerate than having them addressed directly. To a child's magical way of thinking it sometimes seems that only when they speak about their own fear does it become truly real. Of course this indirect approach shouldn't mean that important psychical material is covered up out of fear during the further course of the therapy, or that we avoid addressing fear. It takes not just tact but also experience to sense the right moment after the establishment of a relationship, when enough confidence has arisen for the child to be able to look his or her fear in the eye and talk about it with the therapist.

One particular question is how far and in how much detail we can discuss the result of the interview with parents. First of all, it is undoubtedly an advantage to be able not only to report to the parents what was important in the interview and what conclusions we have drawn from it, but also to show them the course of the interview, and particular important points, directly through the pictures. It is often the case that the pictures are very convincing—indeed, deceptively so—and this means that the parents are willing to follow the therapist's thoughts as he explains them with reference to particular pictures drawn by their child. However, there are several reasons for not being too optimistic here. In the first place, there is no guarantee that parents who agree straight away with our interpretation have really understood what the child's problems are all about. Sometimes, indeed, an instant agreement may express a much deeper refusal to concern themselves with these things at all. This may extend to the parents looking at the "nice" pictures and hardly listening to what the therapist thinks the child is expressing in them. They may show little inclination to think further about the problems, difficulties and contradictions connected with the pictures.

On the other hand, pictures of this kind can represent such impressive experiences for parents as to make them suddenly able to see their child in a new light and behave differently towards him or her. Or they begin to think about things to do with themselves and their relationship with and perception of their child, and about their own fears and limitations, and thus become able to initiate a development process together with the child. This can of course only happen if the parents are willing and able to create a reasonably supportive and stable environment for their child and can provide adequate support for his or her development. In cases where this support is in doubt, careful consideration would be required before communicating such intimate details to the parents, but this would not be a contra-indication for the use of the squiggle game itself.

There are parents with a history of inner conflict resulting from their own experience of trauma and abuse, who have a tendency to control or abuse their child or treat him or her with disinterest and contempt for their person. Such parents naturally also tend to misuse any insights which the therapist has gained from working with the child. As soon as a conflict arises, there is a danger that the material will be used to humiliate and expose the child, and to project onto the child all the badness they feel in themselves and find unbearable. In such constellations we should be extremely cautious about what we communicate specifically about the interview, and should always bear in mind that some extraordinarily sensitive parts of the child's self, the child's deep insecurities and conflicts may have come to light in it.

For this reason I always ask the children beforehand whether they agree to our looking at the pictures together with the parents. In most cases the children are even eager to show their squiggle pictures to their parents and to explain them—presumably because their minds are occupied with the fact that these are no ordinary pictures but ones with close links to deep inner processes. Nevertheless, the explanations the children give their parents are often very simple and oriented to the manifest content, so that it is generally left up to me to present the inner richness and the core of the problems in such a way that the parents can grasp them. Whether it is better to do this with everyone present or in a separate interview with the parents has to be decided in each particular case, and will depend on the therapist's preferences and also to a great extent on the age of the child. The interview with the parents after a squiggle interview is thus no different from any other such exchange after interviewing a child.

What exactly, one might ask, is the difference between a squiggle interview and a normal one, whether with a child or with an adult? Nothing fundamental, certainly, except perhaps that we are made constantly much more aware that this type of interview is about subjective meanings and not objective facts. Winnicott wrote on this subject: "It is of no great value to know facts from the mother, and a patient's answers to questions lead nowhere except away from the central theme, which in psychiatry *is always a difficult one* and in fact is always the place *where the conflict is exactly to be found*" (Winnicott, 1971a, p. 63, italics in the original). In this respect it is true that a therapeutic interview with a child and one with an adult do not differ in principle.

The analogy goes much further. In the first interview with an adult, too, there is a constellation of scenes which go far beyond language-based communication and which enact unconscious conflicts. Hermann Argelander has studied this intensively in his little book *Das erste Interview in der Psychotherapie* (1970), and I would like to present briefly those of his points that touch on our theme. It is clear that first interviews with adults present us with very similar questions to those we meet in squiggle interviews with children. Argelander starts from the observation that precisely in such first interviews, what is said and what happens are amalgamated in an unusual form in the situation. He speaks of a creative ability to stage unconscious conflicts in dramatic form, which he regards as an admirable human talent and even as a specific ego function, the "scenic ego function".

The essence of psychological illnesses lies in unconscious inner psychical processes which can be unlocked in a current "scene" staged with the person spoken to. We know that the patient will already let this come to light in the first interview with the help of a scenic ego function, and we should wait until our understanding co-ordinates with it pre-consciously. [Argelander, 1970, p. 61]

He goes on to say that the situation created by the patient attains a significance of its own as a medium of communication because it gives a particular meaning or a certainty of meaning to the contents of the interview. A situation of this sort, in which a patient can not only communicate and express himself but also reveal his inner conflicts, has to be created actively by the therapist. This is done above all not only by respecting such a staging of scenes but also by initially giving the patient the opportunity to be active. The patient's wishes and demands should be accommodated as far as the therapist's reality will allow. For example, we should recognize that the patient has a right to ask for an urgent appointment and then not turn up for it, only to make contact again six months later. This offers the patient the opportunity to bring his conflict into the situation.

> The sole intention of the interviewer to understand the patient encourages the patient to put aside everyday experiences of conversations and his customary reserve in them and let himself go with the unusual character of the situation. In a first session the interviewer does not criticize or judge. He takes everything as it comes and is only concerned with searching for its meaning ... Most patients experiencing this attitude will open up surprisingly quickly, and speak with relief of things they would not normally share with anybody. This attitude, expressed in quiet waiting, in suspended attention and in showing interest, has a decisive influence on the depth of the conversation. [*ibid.*, p. 43]

The elements are the same ones we met in thinking about squiggle interviews: the stress on the subjective meaning of what is communicated, the creation of an atmosphere in which two people can have a mutual exchange, faith in the creative staging of unconscious conflicts and finally—as an important element of the whole—the unusual and the surprising character of what happens. Another vital element is the ability to wait quietly and not give interpretations too quickly, to obtain the patient's unconscious confirmation of every interpretation offered, and not to confront the patient with "a comprehensive explanation of the therapist's view of the meaning of the illness" but limit oneself to "comments, interpretations or questions which reflect only the meaning of the current phase of the conversation. Every single phase of the interview will be examined in this way for its unconscious content, including the dramatic moment in the situation itself." (*ibid.*, p. 57) Argelander, too, assumes that it is the patient who guides the perception of the interviewer.

The examination of striking, unpleasant, seemingly unproductive phenomena can lead to the therapist receiving unusual answers and being able to recognize connections which are far more revealing than answers to a whole catalogue of direct questions to the patient. The common anxiety of interviewers that they may obtain insufficient material if they do not collect enough data is completely unfounded; in his view, the opposite is the case. The mass of data, particularly the "dramatic" data of unconscious communications, is generally more that the interviewer can assimilate. He often cannot register and integrate the multiple layers of the patient's communications to create a clear picture of the patient and his psychical state. The interviewer needs (and here we find parallels to Winnicott's ideas on squiggle interviews) to have "a clear concept and sophisticated technique in order to reflect on the interplay of subliminal tensions in the reactions of the two participants in the interview and to integrate them with other data" (*ibid.*, p. 21).

This view, that creative staging of scenes in a first interview gives key information to help us register what is going on in someone else's psyche, comes very close to our own view of work with children using a squiggle interview. The dramatic dynamics of staging a scene draw on unconscious sources in the same way as the process of squiggle drawing does. In a well-directed interview with a patient who is not in a state of agitation, this staging will proceed below the surface, and it requires well-trained perceptions to make productive contact with it. This too can be applied to the squiggle interview, where it is also a case of limiting activity to drawing and talking together. The dramatic staging of unconscious conflicts will, if all goes well, develop within this framework and not in manifest acting out, which might even break through the boundaries of the situation. But here too, there is a danger of being carried away by the dramatic element, which can take over the stage completely and lead the patient and the interviewer to act out, to deal with inner conflicts in actions. Winnicott seems to have the more dynamic understanding of this inner conflict, when he points out that it is necessary to allow a little chaos and as a therapist to enter into the spirit of it, while at the same time introducing an element of structuring. In contrast, Argelander emphasizes that with adults, if the interview takes an unfavourable course, the latent dynamics may take over in the form of action and completely flood the scene. According to him, this is the case "when action and joining in the action takes over from communication of insights through language, i.e. when the scene degenerates" (*ibid.*, p. 70).

A warning against the circumvention of defences, against the risk of robbing patients of the protection of their resistance, thereby triggering a dangerous process, is justified for an interview with an adult which chooses an approach of this depth; an admonition to be tactful and cautious, letting the patient decide how far he or she wishes to go is equally justified for a squiggle interview with a child. With children and adolescents, as with adults, it is a question of clinical experience and the ability to hold back. I regard it as essential to find the right balance in each individual case, avoiding on the one hand the risk of denying inner conflicts and of manic resistance, and on the other hand the danger of circumventing the well-grounded defence formations which protect against all too powerful fears and so help to maintain the patient's ability to work in therapy. Nevertheless, I find myself unable to offer any general rules for guidance in this question. The most important thing is presumably to remind ourselves constantly to listen to the patient without letting the prejudices acquired in theoretical study and clinical experience influence us too much; at the same time we must tolerate the fact that we understand very little at first—in fact, in the session we might not even be able to formulate properly the inklings of understanding that we do pick up, instead bringing them into the conversation rather awkwardly. In any event, we should not let ourselves be tempted by the stimulating qualities of the squiggle game into thinking that enough experience, common sense and personal intuition will enable us to work with it, and that we might replace knowledge of the subject, professional experience and solid training with the uninhibited character of this game.

Winnicott's name is often connected with the concept of the squiggle game, and the term appears in numerous publications about him, though there is no actual report on the work done with it. There is a Squiggle Foundation which is dedicated to spreading practice and maintaining interest in Winnicott's work. But here too the term stands for his complete work, not specifically the work he did with the squiggle game. Similarly, the squiggle game is quite widely used in practice by child psychoanalysts, psychoanalytically-oriented child psychiatrists and child psychotherapists, but relatively little has been published on the subject. I can only speculate as to why there is such a discrepancy. One reason might be the highly unusual inclusion of the therapist as subject and the disclosure of this in a publication. The feeling that in their own squiggle pictures they are laying bare the way they work and react in the diagnostic and therapeutic process might perhaps deter a few potential authors. Compared with a purely verbal description of a therapeutic process, we may feel less able to show our theoretical perspective of the process to advantage, and we may feel more directly exposed to the reader's potentially critical eye. What makes this work fascinating for readers—being able to reconstruct for themselves, reflect on and assess the process developing through dialogue between child and therapist (in fact, what science and the communication of clinical knowledge rather impressively claim to do)—may be precisely what makes some authors hesitate. I imagine that Winnicott's warning against objectifying the procedure into a form of test at least implicitly reflected and addressed this problem. For him, the point was precisely to depict the richness of the clinical encounter with the patient in all its subjectivity and so make psychoanalytic work with children communicable and teachable in a new way: teachable not in the sense of offering a fixed canon of knowledge, but in the sense of handing presumably critical readers material to stimulate their thinking, material with which to develop their practice further.

A second point gradually became clearer to me in the course of writing this book. It is also formulated by Winnicott, and I have already quoted some of his formulations on this point. The squiggle game is not in itself something we can learn and it is not something about which we need write a lot of clever thoughts if we are interested in the description of clinical work. It is simply a fantastic resource which can facilitate the development and description of a process. It is something that any two people can do with one another, through which they can enter into a relationship, and which they can simply enjoy. It is quickly learnt, and comes to life straight away from the spontaneous gesture which brings it about. What is really needed is the therapeutic armoury: the deep-seated knowledge in the therapist's bones of how the child's psyche develops, and the associated ability and willingness to tune in to communications from the patient even if these are not understood by the patient him- or herself, even when they may be twisted, frightening and initially hard to empathize with. It has to do with a curiosity about what will happen next, a curiosity about what we have not yet encountered, about what we have not learnt despite all our years of therapeutic experience, and about what the child can tell us if we give him or her space to do so.

In this respect it is also hard to write about the squiggle game: we have to write about something we have only just begun to understand or haven't yet understood in order not to miss the point of the game. How much can we write about something we don't yet fully understand? How much can we write about the moment of surprise without boring the reader? The basic attitude demanded by this game has a lot to do with what Bion meant when he said that the analyst has to empty himself of all positive knowledge when he wants to listen to the patient and enter into a relation with him. It has to do with what Bion called K, the activity of knowledge and thus one of the basic ways in which objects can be linked. I hope that in each of the cases reported in this book I have succeeded in bringing to life the unique and unrepeatable encounter with the child, and in sharing with the reader how reflection can spring from the moment of surprise and lead to a deeper understanding of the child's problem.

At this point I want to mention and briefly present a few works which are directly concerned with the squiggle game in order to give the reader the opportunity to encounter views different from my own, and perhaps follow them up. Most of my own published papers on this subject (Günter et al, 1997; Günter, 2000; Günter, 2003) have been incorporated in this book. I have considerably revised some of them for this purpose. Some of the central thoughts in this book were already developed in them.

In his reflections, Bürgin (1992) emphasizes above all the relationship between patient and therapist and the dialogue between them. He sees it as particularly important to discover how far movement or development in the patient's emotions is possible in the diagnostic-therapeutic interview. Such development serves to indicate the patient's ability to enter into a psychoanalytic-psychotherapeutic process. He illustrated his fundamental thoughts with the help of two case vignettes in which he conducted first interviews using the squiggle game. In his thoughts on the squiggle game, he referred to passages in Winnicott which reported that blocks in development could be loosened or ideally transformed into a continuation of the development process, and the child could gain an insight into what psychotherapeutic work could be like.

Bürgin points out above all that considerable demands are placed on the psychotherapist, since rapid and far-reaching identifications and de-identifications with the patient are required. He sees the risk of the therapist bringing his own projections into the material and of the patient's defences being circumvented. What is special about an understanding dialogue with the child in a psychical examination, where the therapist is not purely an observer but a partner involved in the interaction, is that the therapist offers a particular receptivity of a kind totally new to the adolescent or the child. Bürgin stresses that what is said changes with the specific way it is heard and understood, acquiring a new context. In this way the child can begin to understand something of the complex emotional processes involved and discover his or her very own truth.

In the first of the two cases he describes, the squiggle game served to deepen the dialogue after he had already built up a first contact with the boy. The squiggle shows how very much the nine-year-old boy was preoccupied with sexual arousal: this was manifested directly in the drawings. The squiggle dialogue enabled him to define more precisely the boy's level of ego function and ability to undergo therapy. In the second case, Bürgin describes how he used the squiggle game with a 14-year-old boy to try and clarify whether his was a case of debility, pseudo-debility or near-psychotic process. The development in the formal qualities of the pictures—from a threatening, incomplete and lifeless skeleton to an interactive scene involving two living beings—showed how the patient used the dialogue the therapist offered to further his development. In this case the interview gave indications of retardation with pseudo-debility. At the same time the impairment of the physical self was also an important theme.

The use of drawing in the interview encourages many children to depict problematic themes connected to their relationship with their own body. Above all, this inclination can be observed very clearly in children with physical illnesses, and can be of value in their therapy. In Winnicott's book *Therapeutic Consultations in Child Psychiatry*, the first case is nine-year-old Iiro, who depicted the inner conflicts stemming from his malformed hand and the resulting fears and relational conflicts in pictures of strikingly expressive character. I had similar experiences as a consultant at the Paediatric Clinic, particularly when I worked with children suffering from life-threatening diseases who, for instance, had to undergo chemotherapy for cancer, and so along with pronounced physical distress also experienced changes in their appearance, which for them was linked closely to existential fears. The representation of a person's own body in these scenes is often very closely connected to the question of their own identity (Günter, 1995).

Eight-year-old Oliver had refused to continue therapy in the Life Island, a kind of isolation cell protecting him from infection, in which he had to spend several weeks in order to have a bone marrow transplant. He wrecked his room, threw syringes at the doctors and nurses, and finally, in one of these fits of fury, went out of the Life Island, creating a life-threatening situation due to the risk of infection. I was called in the next day, and suggested that we play the squiggle game. From my squiggle he made a figure (fig. 1–1) and wrote on it "Tha's you", clearly a projection that made it easier for him to meet me on one level and to push his own situation away from himself. What was unmistakable was the missing hair caused by the

Fig. 1–1: Oliver (8), Tha's you (sic)

chemotherapy (the ears appeared very large as a result), the rubber glove which represented his only direct contact with the outside world, and the cross in one ear as a sign of the possibly fatal outcome of his therapy. The mouth, which played a central role in the subsequent picture dialogue between us, was missing here. Oliver addressed this himself, saying that he couldn't get the mouth in right. Physically, it was his lips, mouth and mucous membranes that were most perceptibly affected by the chemotherapy—his lips were cracked and the inside of his mouth was stinging. However, the depiction of his body pointed above all to this boy's psychological situation: he had nobody who could understand him, to whom he could talk about his fear of death, his anger and his despair. After we had talked about these, the boy was visibly relieved and worked as hard as he could with the therapy.

Branik (2002) also described this close connection in one of his case vignettes. Within the framework of the squiggle game the 16-year-old patient soon touched on his inadequacy, his sexuality and his sexual identity. The game culminated in a picture of a tiger lying on its nose as a bedside rug. Branik interpreted the boy's last picture as an expression of the physical changes occurring in puberty, and concluded from the course of the conversation that he had to help the boy to integrate his sexual body into his image of himself instead of hating it as a source of psychological pain. From this Branik developed possible ways of approaching the adolescent patient's use of the body in staging scenes, and of using this in therapy.

In another paper, Branik (2001) showed the usefulness of the squiggle technique for interviews particularly to help understand psychotic processes and their relational dimension. With the help of a squiggle interview and drawings it was possible for a 12-year-old patient to convey to the therapist themes which disturbed him deeply. He did this in part implicitly in the drawings, in part explicitly in the ensuing conversation and commentary. The increase in his ability to function during the course of the conversation gave the therapist reason to hope that an approach to the associated defence processes could be made.

Bürgin (1978), Günter et al (1997), Günter (2000, 2003) and Di Gallo (2000) have all pointed to the significance of the squiggle game as a diagnostic and therapeutic tool in work with children suffering from cancer. As I have already noted, this applies to all children with serious chronic or even life-threatening illness. Their defence organisation often makes it necessary not to approach their inner situation too directly in conversation. Talking too openly would at times bring too many deep-seated fears to the surface and endanger vital defences. The deep narcissistic injury caused by bodily impairment might also come too close to consciousness, and this, particularly in situations of extreme stress, is unbearable for many children. As we have said, in stressful situations of this kind, squiggle games—conducted by sufficiently experienced interviewers—can sometimes be particularly suitable for maintaining an appropriate balance between defence and meaningful communication.

Di Gallo (2000) emphasized above all that the aim of the conversation is to foster the intact ego functions so that the child can maintain the experience of continuity and coherence. The diagnostic and therapeutic dialogue must evaluate the coping and adapting mechanisms available to the child. In his first case study he described how his patient was in the end able to develop their squiggle game into a story which made clear the extent of the threat he felt. Later Di Gallo referred back to this encounter when he looked back, together with the boy, at the drawings done during the time of the boy's treatment in isolation, and continued the therapy. A second case study showed how little the patient was able to draw help from relationships to overcome his cancer and how far he had to resort to magic mechanisms of omnipotence.

In his book on therapeutic work with children who had cancer, Bürgin (1978) showed the importance of squiggle interviews in this type of work. He too emphasized that children are usually extremely irritated by direct questioning, and react to this upsetting of their psychological balance by reinforcing their defensive measures. Blockages in thinking and feeling and obsessive rationalisations gain the upper hand. In contrast, the drawing game, as an offer of relationship and transference with regressive undertones and at the same time of an opportunity for the children to distance themselves, provides an ideal means of entering into a meaningful dialogue with them in such a situation. Thus the squiggle technique facilitates the establishment of a personal therapeutic relationship with the child. Further examples of such work with children in treatment for cancer can be found in Chapters 10 and 11 in this book, and there is further theoretical consideration in Chapter 14.

Brafman (1997) modified Winnicott's technique by inviting children to the diagnostic interview together with their parents. He explored the children's situation using the squiggle technique (along with other means). His starting point was the assumption that the unconscious phantasies of the child interact with the earlier experiences of the parents in a vicious circle. The analyst's role was to help the child to express fears in a form that both child and parents could understand. If the child's unconscious phantasies could be talked about with the help of the squiggle drawings, and as a result the parents could recognize their child's needs, the knot would be undone. Normal development could then continue, provided that the child had not developed a severe emotional disorder.

A further modification was presented by Berger (1980). He adapted the technique of the squiggle game for paediatric practice, thereby actually changing the game's core content of communicating unconscious content through dialogue. He saw the squiggle drawings as a "springboard for discussion with the child", that is to say as a starting point for the conversation, which they can doubtless be even if a deeper investigation of the sense of what the child communicates in his or her drawings doesn't result directly from the squiggle game. Claman (1980) pursued a similar direction, combining the squiggle technique with an exchange of stories. A significant difference from Winnicott's approach lies in the therapist structuring communication much more firmly and directly, and largely refraining from interpretation of unconscious conflicts. Instead of this, Claman used the squiggle drawings to encourage a thematic expression of near-conscious contents.

Scribbled drawings, like drawings in a therapeutic relationship in general, are on the one hand an expression of this relationship between patient and therapist, and on the other hand an expression of an inner process in the patient; they always have something to do with the attempt to find and to try out solutions for problems (cf. Günter, 1993; Baxandall, 1990). At the same time, as pictures they are also subject to the rules of visual perception and aesthetic creation. An aesthetic creation always has to be seen in a historical context which has to do, among other things, with concrete experiences of seeing, in particular with the pictorial conventions of a particular time and culture; it therefore gains a historical and cultural imprint. On the other hand, our sensory perceptions are also strongly determined by innate physiological rules. They seem to present us with a direct copy of the world but in fact always produce a construct of reality. This was already known in principle by 19th century psychologists, and modern neuropsychological research has provided a great deal of evidence for it. Hoffmann (1998), for instance, described in detail the complex rules by which our visual world is set up bit by bit in an interplay between the retina in the eye and complex processes of stimulation in the brain. He showed how our perception of even the simplest lines is underlain by complex construction processes in the brain, the complicated elements of which we are only just beginning to understand. These processes by which perception is constructed—for sight, the construction of visual perception—run continuously at such high speed that we are not conscious of them. It was for this reason that the great 19th century physicist and physiologist von Helmholtz described seeing as a process of "unconscious inference", something which modern neuroscience has been able to prove experimentally down to fine details. The operations carried out in seeing are so complex that nearly half of the cerebral cortex is needed for them.

Now this description of perception as "unconscious inference" has very little to do with the concept of the unconscious as used in psychoanalysis, as it involves more or less purely cognitive perception and construction processes. However, various contributions from the field of neuroscience have also pointed out that visual intelligence is closely connected not only with rational intelligence but also with emotionality.

At a very general psychological level, which is what interests us here, it has long been well known that we tend to project inner memories, affective states and psychological processes into relatively unformed picture shapes. Gombrich (1960) quotes the Classical author Philostratus, who in his biography of Apollonius described a debate between Apollonius and a pupil. They were discussing the shapes seen in the drift of clouds across the sky: centaurs, horned antelopes, wolves and horses. They agreed that the clouds owed their origin to chance but that people gave them shape and meaning, and thus it was the mind alone that created these pictures—precisely in the sense of a projection.

Even Alberti, the great art theoretician and biographer of artists in the Italian Renaissance, attributed the development of art to the human ability to project something into diffuse shapes. In his work on sculpture, *De Statua*, he started from the assumption that at some stage man discovered in a tree trunk, a lump of clay or some other natural material certain outlines that required only slight changes in order to take on an amazing resemblance to a natural object. When men noticed this, they tried to achieve a complete resemblance by adding or taking away, and found that it gave them pleasure when they succeeded. Similarly, Leonardo da Vinci wrote in a famous passage, this time intended as a technical aid to painting:

> You should look at certain walls stained with damp, or at stones of uneven colour. If you have to invent some backgrounds you will be able to see in these the likeness of divine landscapes, adorned with mountains, ruins, rocks, woods, great plains, hills and valleys in great variety; and then again you will see there battles and strange figures in violent action, expressions of faces and clothes and an infinity of things which you will be able to reduce to their complete and proper forms. In such walls the same thing happens as in the sound of bells, in whose stroke you may find every named word which you can imagine.

Leonardo used the power of the imagination and the ability to project into such indeterminate shapes to give the painter inspiration for new ideas. Inchoate shapes such as clouds and muddy puddles had in them the power to spur the mind to new inventions. Leonardo advised artists to avoid the usual methods of careful and precise drawing, since a quickly scrawled, ephemeral sketch could give an artist new ideas. He used the unfinished draft as a screen on which he could project his ideas (quoted from Gombrich, 1960, p. 159).

> Sometimes we see a cloud that's dragonish;
> A vapour sometime like a bear or lion,
> A tower'd citadel, a pendent rock,
> A forked mountain, or blue promontory
> With trees upon't, that nod unto the world,
> And mock our eyes with air . . .

as Shakespeare wrote in *Antony and Cleopatra*, describing the same tendency for projection which would become a recurring theme in art.

In psychology, projective tests (above all the Rorschach form interpretation test), among others, are founded on this principle of the psychology of perception. In particular, the linking of sensations with remembered images and the adaptation of the perceived image to the remembered image (and thus to the inner psychical world of experience) played a decisive role in the original theoretical concept of Rorschach's experiment. This subject has also been intensively studied in Gestalt psychology. Arnheim (1954, 1982) pointed out on several occasions that one should assume that structural features in visual form will be spontaneously related to similar features in human behaviour. He termed this "isomorphic symbolism". This isomorphic correspondence means that something expressed in physical behaviour, such as the gestures of a dancer, appears to be directly understandable to the observer. This was also true, he pointed out, for the flapping of a towel on a washing line or the structural features in the shape of a cloud, whose relatedness to similar structural features in human behaviour, for instance, is perceived directly. If we can assume this for such general fields of experience, we can also expect that the child will choose to depict forms that correspond to his or her own actions (Arnheim, 1982). This reflection casts light again on the tendency I mentioned earlier for many children to concern themselves in their squiggle drawings implicitly or explicitly with depictions of their own bodies and of phantasies about them.

Actually conducting a squiggle interview is relatively straight-forward from an observer's point of view. I usually start with a brief conversation with the child, perhaps asking about his or her situation at that moment and why he or she is there; then I ask whether the child has talked to the parents about seeing me, or about brothers and sisters and school. Often, if the family has come to my surgery, I also talk to the parents and child together, which gives me the opportunity to get an outline of their concerns and reasons for coming to me, and I can perhaps pick up some first impressions of the dynamics of the relationship between parents and child and between the parents themselves.

It may well be that I have already received more information. Particularly if I am called in as a consultant to children with a somatic illness in a paediatric clinic, I will normally have spoken to the doctor and nurses and asked them to tell me why they think the interview is necessary or advisable. In some cases I may conduct the squiggle interview only after two or three normal conversations with the child in order to gain more insight into his or her inner dynamics. As a rule I will also have more information when examining children who are in-patients in our department and are known to me from team discussions. But here too, I first try more or less to forget what I know or think I know about the child and his or her inner situation. I want to be as open and unprejudiced as possible in meeting a child, whether known to me or not, and leave space for what the he or she wants to bring to me.

After this short preparatory conversation, and after I have asked the parents to sit and wait outside, I tell the child that I would like to play a drawing game with him or her. It's quite a simple game: I will make a squiggle on the paper and they are to make of it whatever they like. Then it will be their turn to make a squiggle on a fresh sheet of paper and I will turn it into what I like, and so on. If children hesitate, I encourage them to try it. If they say they can't draw, I point out that I'm not very good at drawing either and it's not important, as it is in school, that the drawing should be good. In most cases children are very soon ready to join in.

I have a stack of A4 paper at hand. Sometimes the children ask if we are going to draw on all these pieces of paper. I answer that we probably won't need them all but we'll just start and see. As a rule I use two different pencils, for instance one plain and one dark coloured pencil: this makes it easier to distinguish afterwards between what the child has drawn and what I have drawn. This is sometimes quite helpful for documentation purposes. If I have to give a lecture on the squiggle game, I am often asked which lines are the child's and which are mine. I have often found that importance is attached to this distinction, but for the game itself and for reflecting afterwards on the child's inner dynamics they don't seem that important to me. It often doesn't particularly matter what figure the child has made out of which particular scribble and exactly what he or she added. The important thing is rather that a dialogue in pictures and words is initiated which allows the child to communicate something of his or her inner state. I won't deny that for certain questions it can sometimes be helpful to know exactly what was drawn by the child. On the other hand, what really is interesting is to see *how* a child draws: whether the lines are thin, tentative and hard to make out or thick, strong strokes; whether the child presses hard enough to tear the paper; whether he or she draws haphazardly and wildly or very slowly and carefully. It is also sometimes revealing to observe whether the child fills the whole sheet of paper or limits him- or herself to one small corner; whether the process of drawing causes the child to open up or to withdraw; whether he or she dares to change, correct or draw over my lines or is anxious to follow my lead. All these things enter my perception and phantasies about the child and his or her inner life, and can sometimes offer important indications. After the event it is usually not so critical to be able to follow all this in detail; it is certainly more important to note the atmosphere of the interview, the counter-transferences produced, and what was discussed.

One crucial element in conducting the squiggle game is that the therapist must provide an atmosphere in which the child feels accepted, in which they can experience a serious discussion of their situation. On the other hand, the outer frame should be kept fairly elastic. This means, for instance, that I don't insist that we always take turns. On the contrary, if the child shows an inclination to draw a picture out of their own squiggle, I encourage them to do so. It's also not a problem if they want to add something to my picture, and I take care not to place any limits on them in this respect.

When and in what kind of situation can a squiggle game be applied? In my view, it is in principle applicable in all interview situations, whether in child psychiatry surgeries, in counselling, as a first interview at the beginning of long-term psychotherapy or child analysis, or simply for a paediatrician who would like to get more closely in touch with a child patient. Naturally, the kind of material that emerges and the kind of contact we have with the child will depend greatly on the situation in which we speak to the child, and above all on our background and training. With psychoanalytical training we will be able to reach far deeper into the unconscious layers of a child's inner life, or at least be able to recognize them more clearly, and make contact at the level of unconscious communication in order to work with the child. In this respect we must agree with Winnicott when he says that psychoanalytical training is needed for this kind of relationship-building. On the other hand, this naturally doesn't mean that we can't achieve meaningful contact with the child in a different manner and that the squiggle game wouldn't be helpful in doing so. This kind of dialogue relationship is helpful even in making contact at a more conscious level. Of course, even in a relationship of this kind and in diagnostic and therapeutic work, we can make fuller and more productive use of what we have learnt and what we know if the squiggle game makes it easier to set up the relationship with the child. However, we should not imagine that the medium of the squiggle game will more or less automatically bring about a psychoanalytical interview.

We can therefore use the squiggle game in almost all forms of interview with children. However, as I have already mentioned, it is not appropriate to use it as a continuing method we can repeat as often as we like within the framework of long-term psychotherapy. It is particularly useful with children who are insecure or withdrawn, who for whatever reason react to an examination with rejection. We often observe that children who at first want to have nothing to do with the interviewer will open up quite quickly after accepting the offer of a squiggle game. It is then often possible to make real contact with them within the game, and perhaps win them over for further therapy. A second group of children with whom in my view this is sometimes the only real opportunity to build a relationship is children with a chronic physical illness. These children, particularly if their illness involves severe impairment or is life-threatening, often find it extremely difficult to talk about their experience of illness or their inner situation. They are in distress, and try to ease this distress by denial, which seems to be their only "realistic" option in view of the restrictions and the requirement for them to co-operate with their treatment. These children, who in the course of their illness become experts in it and therefore appear to be trapped in an objectifying attitude to it, can often only express what they are experiencing subjectively through such indirect means of depiction. Thus they are more willing to accept the offer of a squiggle game, which seems less threatening with regard to their defence organisation than allowing themselves to enter into a direct dialogue. Chapters 10 and 11 give examples of squiggle interviews with such children. Little Iiro, the first case described in Winnicott's squiggle book, was also a severely and chronically sick child, who seems to have been able to speak about his inner distress and conflicts for the first time with the help of the squiggle game. Every time I read that account I am moved by the way this boy spontaneously turned

Winnicott's very first squiggle into a duck's webbed foot, and thus immediately brought out his most important problem: syndactilia (a deformity in which the fingers are joined), for which he had already undergone a number of operations.

There are virtually no limitations or contra-indications for the use of the game. The only situation in which is not possible to conduct a squiggle interview is when a child refuses point-blank, which can occasionally happen. We can then try to encourage them and allay some of their fears. But there are situations in which none of this helps and the child continues to refuse. These are often children who—for whatever reason—cannot or will not allow themselves to enter into a therapeutic encounter, whether because they are too scared or because they absolutely refuse to work with any adult outside the family. In some such cases no kind of interview is possible, and we have to invent some other means of communication and treatment. In general, however, children who otherwise refuse to speak are much more willing to open up in a squiggle game, though even then they might not say a lot. Even with cerebral impairment resulting, for instance, from brain injury or a degenerative process, including cases with visuomotor impairment, in my experience we can conduct a squiggle interview. For example, in this book I describe the case of a boy who suffered from considerable neuropsychological impairment and was nevertheless able to depict his inner situation. Mental retardation should also not be regarded as a contra-indication. On the contrary, it is often easier for mentally disabled children to express their inner state through drawings, something they would probably find more difficult to do as clearly in speech.

As to age, the preferred group is usually aged between 5 and 14. But even this should by no means be regarded as a rigid limit, particularly at the upper end of the range. My experience of using the squiggle game with older teenagers and even, on occasion, with adults has been very positive. With teenagers and young adults it is very important to explain that this is not a test of their drawing or educational abilities.

I should like to add a few comments on practical procedure in special cases. As a rule these are situations which can also crop up in one way or another and cause difficulties in other interviews with children, and they may need to be handled in a particular way. One such situation is if a child outwardly goes along with the demands made and follows instructions, but is obviously not willing to enter into a relationship. This can take on a clearly demonstrative character. For instance the child draws very stereotypical things—which can of course also be for other reasons—and it becomes clear that he or she is refusing to open up properly and enter into a relationship with the therapist. This is a situation we need to address, and it may be possible to bring some of the reasons for this refusal to light. For example the child may have reasons to hold on to a deep-seated distrust of any kind of psychically meaningful relationship. A similar case is when the child covers the entire page with scribbles and thus perhaps tries to cover up what he or she might otherwise say.

A slightly different situation is where the child consciously—sometimes even provocatively—makes extra-difficult and complicated squiggles, and may become pleased and excited if they manage to present the therapist with a squiggle he finds difficult to turn into a picture. These are dynamics which often have a lot to do with the contents and relational conflicts that a child wishes to express but at this point is unable to express in any other way. Although such behaviour demonstrates the child's complete ambivalence towards allowing himself to become involved in relationships, on close examination, it represents a coded offer of a relationship. We find such things for example in deprived children with antisocial defences, what Winnicott terms anti-social tendencies. The situation is different again when children use abstract symbols, numbers or letters or sometimes even interpret the therapist's squiggles as finished letters or numbers. This frequently has to do with marked defence structures against deep fears that would be unleashed if any free flow of feelings were allowed. I have often found this form of stabilization and defence against fears particularly in children with life-threatening illnesses. Depending on the way the interview goes, it may be possible to address these defences and interpret them cautiously. Often a window opens in the defence system for a short time: this can be used as a starting point for further treatment. But these children in particular should as a rule be given the opportunity to rebuild their defences, at least at the end of the interview. A variety of reactions can point to defiance, provocation, irritation, fury and fear of relationships. In essence this is no different from what occurs in any other interview, and should be attentively registered and—

depending on the case—also addressed. It would be a mistake to think that the greater openness and approachability of the child in a squiggle interview means that only the positive relational valencies and transference tendencies are triggered. Aggressive and destructive affects are likewise mobilised, and depressive and paranoid phantasies, fears of being abandoned and claustrophobic fears can dominate the dynamics of the relationship.

If the child wishes to end the interview after a short time I usually make an attempt to motivate him a little longer, and this often succeeds. If, however, the child presses to do something else or even to break off the interview, I usually suggest that each of us draws one more picture. In most cases the children agree to this suggestion. One example is five-year-old Paul, who came to my surgery recently because, as his parents reported, he had extreme temper tantrums and also could not tolerate being asked to play with others. He drew a dragon with wings (fig. 1–2) from my first squiggle. After that he wanted me to make a blowfish (fig. 1–3) out of his squiggle, which he had made very complicated, laughing as he did so. This fish would blow itself up to a terrifying size if anyone wanted to eat it and had threatening spines so that this could not happen. He then drew a

Fig. 1–2: Paul (5), Dragon with wings

hippo with a nose (fig. 1–4) and a cheerful polar bear (fig. 1–5), and what was interesting was that they were practically not based on my squiggles at all. It also soon became to clear to me that he was drawing very large, strong animals, and I connected them to his tantrums. After a few pictures he suddenly said he would like to do something else, and I agreed, after hesitating a little and asking

Fig. 1–3: Paul (5), Blowfish

Fig. 1–4: Paul (5), Hippo with a nose

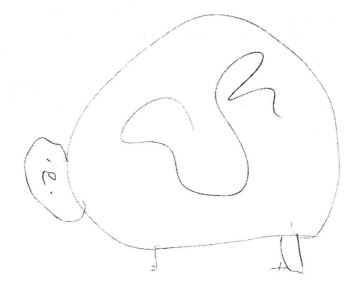

Fig. 1–5: Paul (5), Cheerful polar bear

whether we might each draw one more picture, which he refused. He then played with some small dolls from the toy box and soon displayed a totally different side of his inner world. The story was now about various birds which were extremely threatened. They were either, like a goose, in danger of being eaten by a crocodile, or, like a little chick, in constant danger of sitting on rotten perches and falling off. Paul only played this last scene, which was full of life and made a deep impression on me, after I had commented on how vulnerable some of the birds were. To this he answered that it would be better to keep these things to himself. It was only after I said that I thought he had come here to tell me these stories that he talked about this side of his inner phantasy world. He showed me some of the fear and distress that lay behind the tantrums which helped him to blow himself up into the great big animals of his squiggle drawings. In my view it was important for Paul to keep these two sides of himself well apart even in the examination situation, which he did by switching the medium of play. The presentation of his frightened, needy, powerless side was kept for the game with the dolls and birds, while the omnipotent defence phantasies took shape in the squiggle drawings.

Incidentally, it is my habit to keep the pictures with my papers. In rare cases when the child wants to take the pictures with them I offer to make copies that they can keep.

One particular problem is how to deal with the therapist's own spontaneous thoughts and impulses. Here it is very important to have sufficient capacity for self-reflection, particularly with regard to unconscious countertransference reactions. On the one hand, the ideas should be free and spontaneous so that the associative exchange between child and therapist is supported and no barriers are erected, particularly in this area. There is no dispute in the psychoanalytical literature today about the value of taking into account the therapist's own ideas and countertransference reactions as a significant diagnostic tool. On the other hand, the general rule also applies here: an attitude of suspended attention should help to register what comes from the patient and to examine this material without prejudice. This means that in parallel with allowing free thoughts to come up, it is equally important to refrain from bringing in our own associations too much. It is not always easy to find a satisfactory solution in this paradoxical situation. It seems essential that I hold back, particularly when I become aware of powerful emotional reactions to the material the child produces, which I might be tempted to express in drawing without first reflecting on them. There are moments when a drawing can hurt as much as anything the therapist might say. A drawing can reject a child's needs or even make them look ridiculous. It is also possible for a drawing to relate too directly to an inner conflict, or to represent an attempt to circumvent defences. In all these cases, as with interpretations that seem to ask to be made, the recommended course of action is to exercise restraint and, circumstances permitting, choose a more neutral motif. In interviews I generally try to pay particular attention to what comes from the child, and above all try initially not to let my own themes flow into the pictures too much. However, looking back over a whole series of drawings with different patients, I see that it can't be avoided completely. The therapist, too, has certain psychical, aesthetic and motor patterns which are part of his or her personality.

In any case, towards the end of the interview I make sure I suggest that each of us does one more drawing, and arrange this so that the child is allowed to draw the last one out of my squiggle. This gives the interview a certain rounding off that the child often takes up and uses. I think it is important to give the child the opportunity to have the last word, as it were. Children often use this moment to say something important or to sum up their inner situation once more. It is also the case, however, that children who are under great stress and operating at the very limit of their ability can often make excellent use of this announcement to reconstruct their defences. In the course of the conversation these defences have often become much less rigid: the children have allowed me, and thereby to a certain extent themselves too, access to their inner conflicts, thus letting them come closer to consciousness. Examples of this will be found in the case descriptions that follow. It is often important to let the child leave the interview with the assurance that they have rebuilt their defensive functions and will therefore be able to deal with reality, however hard it may be, until our next conversation.

What is and remains central with the squiggle game is that although drawing has its own place and value, the therapeutic work will ultimately depend to a significant extent on the verbal dialogue. Speaking is a central element of every therapeutic encounter, and one essential function of the picture dialogue in the squiggle game is to facilitate communication in speech. It is possible to talk about the pictures, it is possible to talk about the inner world through the pictures, and in many cases it becomes possible with the help of the pictures for the child to talk about him- or herself. There are significant differences here. For my children with life-threatening illnesses who had to undergo bone marrow transplants, talking about their own situation remained so threatening that they had to limit themselves to just a few words. Even the freedom to talk about the pictures was limited by this threat in many cases.

On the other hand, there are children who can enter into a genuine dialogue with the help of the pictures. Winnicott reports that he could ask children about their dreams during the squiggle interview and many willingly recounted them. Some therapists ask the children to tell them stories about the individual pictures. This, too, can be a way of encouraging the child to approach describing his inner world. We can even go so far as to ask the children to make up a story about the whole sequence of pictures, though to my mind inventing a coherent story requires a certain introspective and cognitive capability. In the end, as Winnicott has stated, the squiggle game is a fascinating, sometimes exhausting, sometimes even seductive means of entering into a relationship with a child, and as such something I would hate to do without in my child psychiatric, psychotherapeutic and psychoanalytic practice. I hope you will find as much inspiration in the following case descriptions as I did in the course of the squiggle interviews.

CHAPTER TWO

Gifts from an angel: will there be rescue from danger?

Fabian, aged 12

Fabian came to me with his mother after missing three months of school; in fact he had not attended since the Carnival holidays. He developed attacks of dizziness in the mornings and collapsed as soon as he tried to leave for school. During the holidays he had no problems. He was described as totally changed: withdrawn, in no mood to do anything, showing very little initiative. Previously he had been lively and outgoing, got involved in everything, and seemed to have no problems. The family couldn't understand the change at all.

They came to me after I had seen Fabian's identical twin brother Benedikt a few times a good year earlier. Benedikt had been described by his school as autistic. In fact he had fallen into a deep depression after his brother Fabian had transferred to an academic secondary school (*Gymnasium*), while he had only been given a recommendation for the less academic *Realschule*. I had discussed the situation with Benedikt and his parents, and we had decided that although the teacher's opinion of his performance was justified, it might be worth trying to place him in a parallel class at the *Gymnasium*. Benedikt had flourished there and had developed really well psychologically, also achieving pretty steady academic results. This led the mother to say that the boys had changed over, as it were, and now Benedikt was lively and outgoing while Fabian was virtually in the state Benedikt had been in before.

I knew from our earlier contact that the mother was a teacher and the father a doctor. There was a friendly, attentive atmosphere in the family, though they were more inclined to try and overcome any problems by tackling them in a practical and energetic manner, and to regard any deeper discussion of inner processes with some scepticism. Nevertheless, both parents were very concerned about their children and willing to discuss the situation, even against their own inclination to overcome life's problems in an active manner.

After a short talk with both the mother and Fabian, I asked her to take a seat in the waiting room and suggested to Fabian that we play a squiggle game. He laughed while I made my first squiggle, and drew a monster (fig. 2–1) out of it, pointing out in particular the eyes and the teeth. When I made a fish (fig. 2–2) out of his squiggle he laughed again. I had the impression that he was quite insecure and fearful.

The next thing he drew was an angel (fig. 2–3). I noticed that under the angel's wing there was a line criss-crossed by a wavy line, and asked him what this meant. He explained that he wanted to draw an arm but it hadn't turned out right. I commented that it looked like an Aesculapian staff, linking this to the fact that his father was a doctor. He said he didn't know what an Aesculapian staff was. It's Christmas, he said (in fact it was spring), and angels come and bring presents and then go back again. They would bring presents for

Fig. 2–1: Fabian, Monster

Fig. 2–2: Fabian, Fish

Fig. 2–3: Fabian, Angel

everyone, small ones and large ones, he explained when I asked him about this. I had a vague memory that some time before this interview with Fabian I had heard in passing that the mother had contracted cancer, and this came back to me now. I was struck by the purposeful way Fabian had steered towards this theme, although in our short conversation before the interview neither he nor his mother had said a word about it. So it seemed that the theme of our conversation was to be the threat to the mother and how she might recover, though I didn't at this point know how the whole thing would develop.

Out of his next squiggle I drew a pillow and added a bed (fig. 2–4). I had commented on the angel's untidy mop of hair and wanted perhaps to signal to him with my picture that there might be a place where he could rest. Fabian drew a sailing boat (fig. 2–5) from my squiggle, its sail filled with wind. Its bow was pointing upwards and it had a rather puny outboard motor.

> Fabian: A sailing boat.
> Self: And the wind is filling the sail?
> Fabian: Yes, and that's the outboard motor.
> Self: Have you ever been on a sailing boat?
> Fabian: No, but I have been on a motor boat on Lake Constance.

I saw this, in reaction to his earlier picture and my offer, as a narcissistic defence in the sense of emphasizing the phantasy of

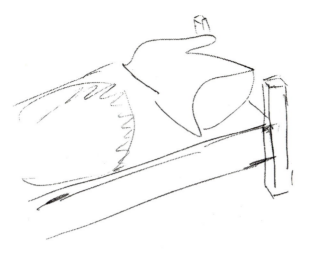

Fig. 2–4: Fabian, Bed and pillow

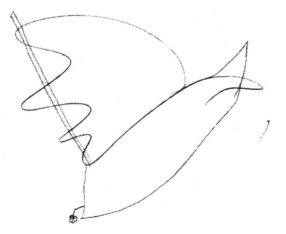

Fig. 2–5: Fabian, Sailing boat with wind-filled sail

moving on, of turning to the future in order to be able to leave these stressful, threatening things behind. Only the puny outboard motor might, like a wedge, perhaps even like a cancerous tumour, hinder rather than help progress. Identifying with his narcissistic defence, which was in a way quite helpful, I made his next squiggle into a dumbbell (fig. 2–6) being lifted by a hand. He laughed and said he

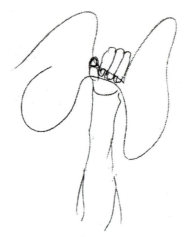

Fig. 2–6: Fabian, Dumbbell

liked it, particularly the hand. But at my next question he immediately withdrew again.

Fabian continued with a man wearing a cap (fig. 2–7). When I asked him to tell me a story about this man he was quite happy to start, even though he had been rather taciturn before. This was a sailor who went to sea in a big ship and then went under. They had hit a block of ice. A lifeboat came and rescued them all, but this man was drowned because he wasn't wearing a life-jacket. I said: "Now we've had first the monster, a dangerous thing, then the angel who can save people, and now another catastrophe where rescue comes but still one person goes under. He looks quite young still, doesn't he?" No, he was quite old, ninety or so. Fabian now came back to the important point and said it was a dangerous ice-block that had rammed the boat, which in his previous picture had been sailing

Fig. 2–7: Fabian, Man with cap

along so powerfully with the wind in its sails. Everyone was rescued except the sailor who had no life-jacket on. The idea crossed my mind that he might be the sailor sailing off to sea, joining the mother and going under with her.

My next picture came out of this atmosphere: it was an earth house with doors and windows (fig. 2–8), representing a protective and stable mother-identification. He drew a car (fig. 2–9), and I sensed that he was hesitant and on the defensive. We talked a bit about this car and he explained that it was an unusual car because it had a spoiler at the back so that he (sic!) would stay firmly on the ground. It also it had an aerial on top for listening to the radio. I asked him

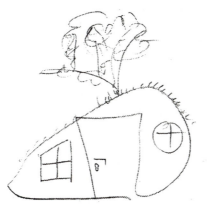

Fig. 2–8: Fabian, Earth hut

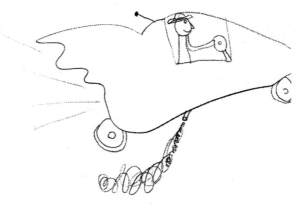

Fig. 2–9: Fabian, Car

about the exhaust, mounted rather strangely in the middle of the car, which I saw as belonging to the little man in the car like a kind of penis. He didn't want to say anything about the exhaust.

Presumably this second set of problems just emerging here, in a conflict around his male identification at the start of puberty, was something which seemed too difficult for him at this point, particularly as it was probably too closely connected with the other problem, the concern over his mother who was threatened by a fatal illness. But we also have to relate it to the rivalry with the twin brother, who had now taken over the leading position, while Fabian, having been ahead for so long, had now fallen behind. Looking back on it, I am impressed with the way different motifs were densely interwoven in this squiggle. The car, which seemed to be taking off by virtue of the exhaust-phallus, had also been given a spoiler to keep him firmly on the ground. And it also had an aerial for listening to the radio, perhaps, we might suppose, to hear what the analyst would say about it.

I drew a face (fig. 2–10), perhaps the face of the little man in the car. Fabian made a hobby-horse out of my squiggle (fig. 2–11), but in the form of a dog. He had always preferred playing with Lego or Playmobil, while his friend had had a hobby-horse like this, when they were five. I understood this to be a regressive step pulling back from the taking-off movement of the car, taking him back into a childish world, while the aggressive and dangerous moments remained represented by the dog's teeth. Next, Fabian drew a

Fig. 2–10: Fabian, Face

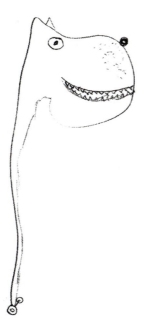

Fig. 2–11: Fabian, Hobby-horse

squiggle which I felt was intended to be difficult for me to make anything from. He may unconsciously have wanted to make it clear to me that we were faced with a difficult task. I commented on how difficult it was, and finally drew a cat out of it (fig. 2–12). Inwardly I was in fact initially preoccupied with deciding whether or not to draw a crab with two pincers, an idea which had immediately presented itself to me. After thinking for some time I decided against it, as I felt it was too blunt and almost like a surprise attack. But this brought me almost to a state of paralysis, so that I found it very difficult to draw anything. Afterwards I understood this as a compressed moment of unconscious communication about how difficult and potentially paralysing it was for Fabian to deal with his mother's cancer. It was typical that up to now not a single word had been spoken about this and yet it was taking up the central position in our communication.

Out of my next scribble he drew a snake which wanted to eat an animal (fig. 2–13). The animal was peeping out of a hole and the

Fig. 2–12: Fabian, Cat

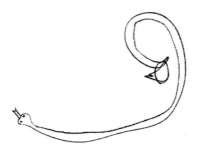

Fig. 2–13: Fabian, Snake wanting to eat an animal

snake wanted to eat it now. At this point I risked coming out with an attempt to talk about what was preoccupying us. I said to him: "I think what I have understood so far it is that it's always about something dangerous and about whether or not rescue will come. So is there maybe something dangerous in your life?"

Fabian: Knives, Dad has an air-pistol and fire.
Self: And for you yourself?
Fabian: There's nothing . . . or rather yes, bangers, Dad took them away. Yesterday Bene [the brother] and I put black powder into a vase and lit it.

Self: And what did you want to do?

Fabian: We wanted to make a volcano.

Self: And was Dad cross about that?

Fabian: Yes, he took the bangers away from us, and Bene went and got them back. Mum was sitting next to us and said we should be careful.

Self: And did you burn yourselves?

Fabian: No.

Self: And with your illness [the dizziness and feeling sick], they didn't really know if it was dangerous or not.

Fabian: No, first they thought it was a gastric infection.

Self: And Mum, isn't she ill?

Fabian: Yes, she had an operation. Then it wasn't better and she went to Hawaii to some bloke who cured her.

Self: Have you been worrying about Mum?

Fabian: No, not much.

Self: Well, I would feel bad in the morning if I had to go to school because I'd be away from Mum for such a long time. But of course I don't really know if there's any reason to be worried about your Mum.

Once again the theme of danger had been taken up. I grasped the opportunity and spoke fairly directly to him, making a link between his school-phobic symptoms and his mother's illness. He did then take this up briefly, telling me that after treatment that he thought hadn't worked, his mother had been to Hawaii to a healer who had cured her. The interesting thing was that he had come to his appointment with me wearing a T-shirt with Hawaiian motifs, which his mother had brought back from Hawaii. His introduction of the bangers made clear the extent to which the whole thing had become tangled with the oedipal-pubertal problem area, the rivalry with his father and the jockeying for position between the two twins, thus becoming extremely difficult. However, in my interpretation I did not touch on this facet of the conflict, particularly the oedipal wishes and related castration anxiety. To interpret and work through this would have required longer therapy.

At this point I suggested that each of us should do one more drawing, and made a tadpole out of his squiggle (fig. 2–14). I feel that with this picture I implicitly addressed the theme of the change

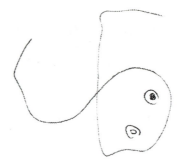

Fig. 2–14: Fabian, Tadpole

from boy to man in puberty, something I had deliberately left out in talking to him. In his final picture Fabian drew a monster with teeth, sticking out its tongue (fig. 2–15). It was a dangerous monster, he said. Here too, I was impressed by the way danger was closely connected to phallic content. After our interview Fabian was anxious to show his pictures to his mother. Essentially, however, he simply named the pictures without explaining in detail what they were about.

Fabian was a boy who was extremely reserved and found it very hard to express his opinions in conversation. The squiggle interview helped him to describe his problems, which enabled me then, with

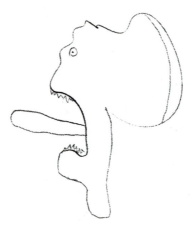

Fig. 2–15: Fabian, Monster with teeth sticking out its tongue

Fabian's permission, to use the pictures in discussing things with his mother. She now told me that she had contracted breast cancer when the boys were nine months old. She had undergone surgery and it had all gone well. She said of herself that she was an expert at putting things out of her mind, and had soon taken up sport again. The children would certainly not have noticed much then. Last summer, about nine months ago, she had contracted uterine cancer. The doctors had recommended chemotherapy and radiation treatment, but she had refused. They had agreed on a hysterectomy, which would remove the need for further chemotherapy or radiation. This time too, she had overcome the problem with sport. Over the Carnival holiday she had flown out to Hawaii to be treated by a spiritual healer. This had done her a lot of good, and she had told the children about it. After these holidays Fabian had stopped going to school, she was now able to tell me.

I was now in a position to discuss the connection between her illness, the insecurities aroused by it and finally her journey to Hawaii and Fabian's school phobia. We were able on this basis to discuss what needed to be done next, deciding on the one hand to set up some specific support with regard to Fabian's school attendance and on the other hand to agree with him that he should come and see me on a weekly basis for the time being. With this support, which also involved his father, Fabian returned to school fairly quickly. The fits of dizziness and social withdrawal gradually disappeared, as did the depressive moods. Until after the summer holidays he came to see me regularly, but said that he couldn't really confirm the connection I had made between his mother's illness and his school phobia in the sense of an anxiety reaction. But he wanted to carry on coming to see me. However, he would like to play billiards with me in the session. After about 15 sessions altogether, which we spent mainly in the rivalry of billiards games, and during which I occasionally dropped in comments on his fears connected with his mother's illness, we were able to end our sessions. Fabian has developed well since then, has taken up his social contacts in school and sport, and both he and his mother feel that the crisis has been overcome.

This is a typical example of how with the help of a brief intervention a knot could be untied and blocked development opportunities could be freed. It is clear that in this case it didn't matter too much whether interpretation of unconscious connections could also be accepted at the conscious level. What seemed to be most important here was rather that Fabian had found a space with me in which such a connection could even be thought of as a possibility. This eased the burden on him to a certain extent, even though in the end he held on to the way in which his family dealt with inner distress: he insisted on competing with me, on a kind of trial of strength, but in return allowed me occasionally to talk about strange things like feelings and inner processes.

It is important as a rule—as this case vignette clearly shows—to concentrate on one theme. Certainly it would have been sensible and necessary in longer-term treatment to work through the marked oedipal rivalry, which was so obvious even in this first interview and was presumably also closely connected with twin rivalry. We may also have to address this problem in such a first interview if we gain the impression that it is significant at the moment. More frequently, however, the general rule is to decide on one central theme and see if some movement in psychical organisation can be achieved in this one area. This does not preclude a decision on more intensive and comprehensive therapy, which can be considered at leisure after reflecting on the material, and then suggested to the child and the parents.

The squiggle game was also important for the mother and her understanding of the boy. As hard as she tried, it was difficult for her—as she herself admitted—to deal with difficult feelings otherwise than through activity. I am convinced that having actual pictures to look at made it easier for her to deal with her son's conflicts in connection with her illness and with the sibling rivalry.

CHAPTER THREE

Whale, camel or giraffe with a balloon of a tummy?

Anne, aged 12

A nne was a twelve-year-old girl who suffered from severe anorexia and depression, and was therefore admitted as an in-patient for treatment in a paediatric clinic. There they had been able to achieve a very slight increase in her weight but, despite intensive psychotherapeutic interviews and an additional course of antidepressant medication, no real change in her eating habits or in her markedly depressive mood. Thus the family and Anne herself decided to agree to longer-term psychotherapeutic treatment in our children's ward.

The girl was described as being reserved, somewhat withdrawn and slow to make contact from early childhood. She had attended a child day care centre from the age of two, but had soon lost any friends there. When she was three she had made friends with a little boy and apparently the two of them were inseparable. She herself referred to this friend as her bridge to the other children. In her early childhood there were also relapses into insecurity and dependency at times of conflict, possibly also after the birth of her sister, who was four years younger. The father said that the mother had insisted on Anne making independent decisions at an early age, which was too much for her. On the other hand, the parents described her as very sthenic and well able to get her own way. For example, at the age of three, when her mother tried to help her get dressed, she had taken off all her clothes and got dressed again herself.

What had triggered the initially severe depressive symptoms was leaving the child day care centre which she had attended for ten years. In the foreground she had feelings of emptiness, weariness and sadness. The symptoms worsened progressively until her condition became life-threatening due to her refusal to eat and finally even to drink. When I subsequently looked through the reports, it struck me that there was not a single word about her sexual development in any of them.

Anne and I arranged a squiggle interview. I explained to her that as the consultant responsible for this ward I would like to get to know her a bit better, and so would like to have a talk with her. At the beginning of our conversation there was mention of the fact that she had found everything better in the Paediatric Clinic. She had got used to having one-to-one talks with the woman doctor there. She said her weight went up and down. When I asked, she said it could well be that she became anxious if her weight went too high or too low, so she tried to keep it in the middle. She also briefly mentioned that she had previously often quarrelled with her sister, but now they got on well when she went home to visit.

Anne had a little difficulty deciding which pencil to take, and finally took the sharper one. She was a little hesitant at first, and finally drew a woman's face out of my squiggle (fig. 3–1), but not without making sure that I could recognize what she had drawn. She criticized this face immediately, as if dissatisfied with her drawing, and perhaps also with herself. By contrast, she praised my drawing of two mice (fig. 3–2) as "cool", but then commented that

Fig. 3–1: Anne, Woman's face

they didn't have any ears. So something was missing. I was presumably preoccupied with Anne's somewhat timid behaviour and tried to tune in to it in the form of the mice. Her next picture—and again she assured herself that I could recognize what she had drawn—was of a whale (fig. 3–3). She became a little uncertain when I initially took her whale for a dolphin. We talked then about the fact that the whale was feeling fine as it looked out of the water. It was spraying water out of its hole. My next drawing showed a snake (fig. 3–4). So we were staying with animals.

Fig. 3–2: Anne, Two mice

Fig. 3–3: Anne, Whale

Fig. 3–4: Anne, Snake

For the next picture, she first looked at my squiggle from all sides and then drew with concentration, paying a great deal of attention to details. You couldn't really tell what it was, she remarked, it was supposed to be a camel (fig. 3–5). I encouraged her a little. She went on drawing, and commented that the camel was carrying a load—a carpet and other objects. She said she didn't know exactly what it was carrying, but it was sweating a great deal, and also had to walk into the wind. We talked a little more about the details, for instance about the drops of sweat that looked to me like tears on the creature's head. I remarked that it occurred to me that the camel could almost be the opposite of the whale: the whale was so cheerful and curious as it looked out of the water. Anne agreed with this remark.

From her next squiggle I began to draw a path with a person coming along it, with lumps of rock bordering it in the foreground (fig. 3–6)—probably a continuation of the camel theme. While I was doing this, she said, suddenly becoming quite lively, that she had thought they were hedgehogs. One of them was about to push an apple away. We talked about how it was laying in a store for the winter. Anne now had flushed cheeks and red patches on her neck, presumably a sign of her keen inner involvement.

I wasn't quite sure at this point, but I was thinking that it might have to do with the conflict between wishing for a feeling of safety in a warm nest on the one hand, and a kind of cheeky curiosity and

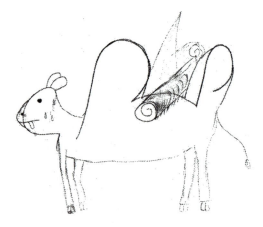

Fig. 3–5: Anne, Camel

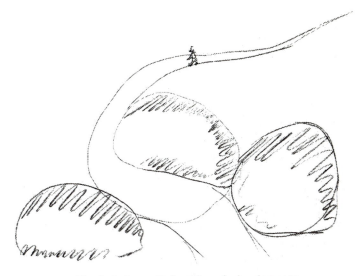

Fig. 3–6: Anne, Path with rocks bordering it

desire to leap out of the water on the other hand. At the same time there was this heavily loaded camel—undoubtedly a picture of her own situation as soon as she tried to set off anywhere. She continued with a "heart-balloon, or a pretzel" (fig. 3–7). When I pointed out to her that there was nobody holding the string, she explained it was simply flying up into the sky. My next picture, a lemon (fig. 3–8), was possibly inspired—without my being properly conscious of it at the time—by the thought of an intense irritation when we

Fig. 3–7: Anne, Heart-shaped balloon or pretzel

Fig. 3–8: Anne, Lemon

encounter something new, something completely unexpected, the way we would be irritated if we bit into a lemon instead of a pretzel. Anne started drawing from my next scribble instantly (fig. 3–9). Finally she explained that she had originally intended to draw a staircase on which a man is coming up behind a woman or kicking the woman. But now it occurred to her that the staircase was missing. Somehow the picture made her think of Cinderella. The shoe was stuck to the step, the prince had stuck it there in order to find the beautiful girl. He would take the shoe with him, she said. When I agreed and said that the prince would marry Cinderella, she objected that that wasn't possible, the shoe was still stuck. I suggested that

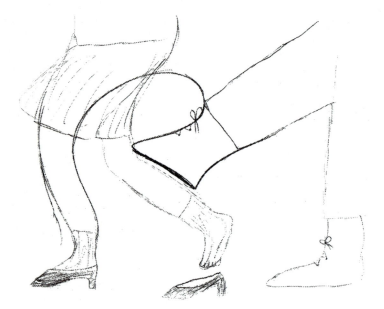

Fig. 3–9: Anne, Cinderella

he might have managed to get it off already. She was silent for a while and then said "but then he's kicking the woman". These were just two people. I interpreted at this point that both might be in Cinderella, as in her pictures. Cinderella was quite homely and had to work hard, and yet she was also the belle of the ball with whom the prince fell in love. The birds helped Cinderella, said Anne, to pick out the peas. It became clear what the drive towards autonomy and the cheekiness, but also the very difficult separation from the bond with the parents was about. Pubescent sexual phantasies played a major role: a man followed a woman upstairs, the man "kicked" the woman, and in the end it became a proper story of transformation with Cinderella becoming a beautiful princess.

The piglet I drew out of her next scribble started quite a discussion (fig. 3–10). She would have made a cap out of it, or it could also have been a bird. The conversation seemed to flow much more freely after the interpretation and was much livelier. In the end she drew a bird on its nest (fig. 3–11). This was a real chick and could flap like one, she said. With this picture we could talk a little more about her desire for independence and the conflicts connected with it, about the whale and the camel. The camel was more how she felt, she said. "But there is still something attractive about it," I objected, and she murmured agreement. And then there's always Cinderella, I said, and she began to laugh. But she hadn't been thinking of anything when she

Fig. 3–10: Anne, Piglet

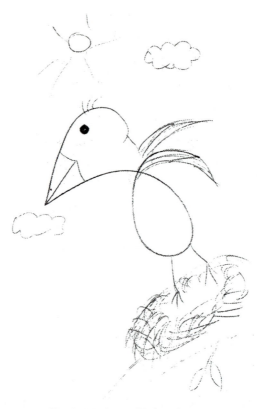

Fig. 3–11: Anne, Bird on its nest

was drawing it, she said. Commenting on her next scribble, she said it looked like the camel in the first picture. I made it into a girl who was dancing (fig. 3–12) and related it to her last but one picture (fig. 3–9). But she's dancing so awkwardly, Anne objected. I confirmed that she still had to learn how to dance. Anne's last picture turned into a particularly beautiful giraffe (fig. 3–13) with a belly as round as a football. We then talked in quite a relaxed way about whether this giraffe was long and thin or whether it had a balloon of a tummy.

In contrast to her extremely reserved, anxious, self-conscious and almost shut-off manner in conversation, in her squiggle drawings Anne showed right from the start that she had another side which was worth discovering, although it also had to do with difficulty and her depression. The desert had almost become reality to her when she had begun to refuse food and even drink. In spite of a family

Fig. 3–12: Anne, Girl dancing

Fig. 3–13: Anne, Particularly beautiful giraffe

history burdened with several suicides and of her extreme symptoms, the approachability she showed and the vitality that came to light gave me hope that we would be able to achieve something within the framework of treatment.

Anne had managed to open up in the course of our work with the squiggle drawings and depict something of her sexual desires and phantasies. This squiggle game shows clearly how important it is for the development of the conversation to leave the initiative to the child, letting her decide what she chooses to reveal about herself and which topics should be discussed. For this to happen, the child must have the feeling that when showing her problems she will encounter an open and receptive atmosphere. It is also important to convey to the child that she can determine the pace of the conversation. Anne's increasing involvement developed over a number of stages. First it was about identification with the desert, the asceticism of her anorexia. It was only after I had entered into this theme with her that she was able to turn her mind cautiously to the opposing wishes in the form of the hedgehogs storing away food, at first in a peripheral way, though linked very closely with her eating problem. Two further steps, the pretzel and the heart-balloon, were needed for her finally to dare approach her secret sexual desires and talk about them through the language of fairy tales. After she had made this the topic of conversation I was, as it were, authorized to carry on talking to her about it. It was then my task to follow it up and address it meaningfully. Her liveliness and the way she became more talkative assured me that I had hit on the right topic and tone in a way that she could use. In this way we were able for a moment to talk in a fairly relaxed manner on the subject of fat and thin on the manifest level, which, we both implicitly recognised, was connected with allowing sexual desires and phantasies of pregnancy. It almost goes without saying that an explicit interpretation of this connection at this point would have been out of place, because it would undeniably have taken on a teacher-like, know-it-all tone, as if the therapist needed to demand from the girl some recognition of his brilliance. In such cases I think it is important to let the squiggle game end unfinished and leave open the possibility of further work: both therapist and child are then curious to know what else will come up. The path onwards will no doubt be mostly stony and troublesome, and we should not let ourselves be deceived by the relative ease of this first encounter. It is not usually possible to work through deeper conflicts in the squiggle game, but nevertheless, if a relationship is established, the conflicts which need to be worked through do for a moment become clearly visible to both patient and therapist.

CHAPTER FOUR

Of pirates and their treasures: the child analyst as archaeologist and treasure hunter

Johannes, aged 10

Johannes was admitted to our children's ward at the age of 10 because of aggressive outbursts both at school and at home, at times combined with very brutal behaviour. At home, his parents said, he threw temper tantrums when he was forbidden to do something or experienced disappointment, and also destroyed things in the process. The relationship between Johannes and his stepfather was very tense on both sides, they said. There was pronounced sibling rivalry towards his half-brothers, who were seven and nine years younger than Johannes, and he repeatedly treated them very aggressively. He had violent quarrels with his mother, and had also stolen quite large sums of money. At school, the situation had become so bad that Johannes was about to be expelled.

I saw Johannes for an interview two days after he had been admitted to our children's ward, and started by asking him why he had come here. His answer was that he couldn't concentrate very well and lost his temper easily. He was already in occupational therapy and speech therapy, he said, so now he was trying this out as well. If this helped him, he would stay; if not he would go back home in four weeks. What kind of temper tantrums did he have? I asked. He smashed things, he said, cars and whatever, if he got annoyed, if someone said something stupid to him, at school or whatever.

I suggested that we play a squiggle game and explained to him how it works. Johannes took up my squiggle immediately and started drawing. "That was once all flooded, a pirate ship (fig. 4–1), and then it went down in a storm. That's under water now. These are rocks [he points to the pointed black spikes down on the sea bed], that's where it came crashing down on top of them and broke apart. And there's also a skeleton, and piranhas are swimming around. There's also a sabre and an axe. And there's a spring, too, and an outlet that runs into a subterranean lake. Will you be saving this picture?" I explained to him briefly that I keep the pictures and also make notes on them. I had a real doctor's handwriting, just like himself, Johannes said. So he had started straight into his theme with the first picture. Chaos, destruction, danger and violence were manifest everywhere in a confined space from which there was no escape—a situation much like the one in which he had obviously become entangled. But there was also this secret spring and outlet to a subterranean lake. For me, it was immediately evident that he was pointing to another side of himself that might be there beneath

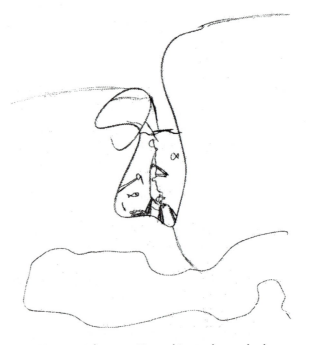

Fig. 4–1: Johannes, Pirate ship on the sea bed

the aggressiveness, destructiveness and despair. Maybe even a bit of hope?

I made an apple out of his squiggle (fig. 4–2), but not without telling him that he had made it difficult for me. Johannes said he would have called his squiggle a work of art and we should frame it. Perhaps this remark already revealed a glimpse of the other side of the confinement conveyed in the first picture: there needed to be a frame for his internal and external chaos, and he might have been suggesting unconsciously that he hoped to find this frame here with us. His comment on my next squiggle was that he could make either a duck or a shoe out of it (fig. 4–3). We could hang that one on the wall too, he said; we could hang it on a hook in the bathroom. Johannes scribbled around again like mad on the next sheet, and I remarked that here was another work of art. I would make a bird out of it, though (fig. 4–4). I could really tell that he wanted to make things as difficult as possible for me. I would have to go back over

Fig. 4–2: Johannes, Apple

Fig. 4–3: Johannes, Duck or shoe

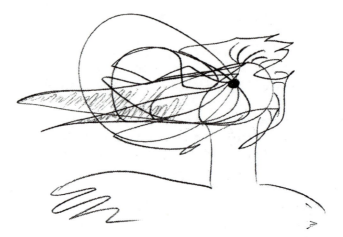

Fig. 4–4: Johannes, Bird

the outlines, he remarked critically; but the bird wasn't bad at all, he generously added immediately.

Seeing my next squiggle, he said that my squiggles always looked similar. And indeed, with deep involvement and loving attention to detail he set about creating a situation that was quite similar to that of the first picture (fig. 4–5). He commented on this connection too, when he asked whether he should draw a stalactite cave or a mountain. "I already have a cave, you know, oh no, that was a lake." A treasure was hidden at the back there, he said, a statue, sort of like a Buddha. There were also "something like spikes in there, from the Mayas, it's almost impossible to get near them". That's all blocked off there, he said, and added some more spikes. Finally, he told the following story: "That's Tilekal, a huge Mayan city. Somebody thought they would explore and find out about the Mayas. And then there's also a stone sarcophagus, the god is in there. There's still some treasure in there." Researchers wanted to go there, and the god was dead, and they worshipped him, he said. He wanted to become an archaeologist too, in Egypt. He had given a talk on it at school once and got top marks for it. At this point I interpreted his wish that we might perhaps also be able to find some treasure in him. Johannes said: "There's also a robber there. He wanted to steal the treasure, then he ran into the spikes, now all that's left of him is a skeleton. That's it! Are you a doctor, can you do

Fig. 4–5: Johannes, Tilekal, a huge Mayan city

stitches too? I hurt myself when I was fishing." Once again, the aggressive-threatening-destructive side was embellished in detail and brought to the foreground, but this time its function was identified: it was there to protect the treasure from falling into the hands of the robbers. There seemed to be a seamless transition between the two. On the face of it, he was the robber who stole money at home and was aggressive. In the story, however, the constellation soon flipped over, and he became the one who was injured and needed the protection and healing art of doctors—possibly at the very moment when I said that there might be some treasure to be found in him too. This was something he obviously no longer expected to hear, having been stuck in a rut for years and been defined by his negative side within the family; but he himself was also in the process of developing a negative identity in Erikson's sense (1956).

I went on to ask whether he liked going fishing and he told me that he did this with his own father. He then told me to do the next squiggle, which he turned into a saxophone (fig. 4–6). His mother played the saxophone, he said. When I asked about his mother, he asked me whether he would get marks for the pictures, and also

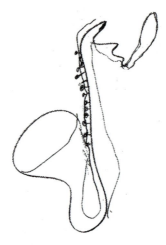

Fig. 4–6: Johannes, Saxophone

asked about my wedding ring. He sometimes played the drums at a friend's house, he added.

On the next sheet, he immediately turned his own squiggle into an old Celtic castle (fig. 4–7). At first he didn't want to say any more about it. It almost seemed as if he had already opened up too much earlier in asking whether I could do stitches, as he'd hurt himself. But finally he did explain that the Romans had razed the Celtic castle to the ground. There were some spikes, and the Romans had smashed into them. The Romans were evil, he said, they had wanted to conquer the whole world, and in the end the Germanic tribes had defeated them. He knew of an old Roman villa nearby. Well, the Celts and the Germanic tribes might have welcomed the Romans, I protested. He laughed out loud at that idea and began telling me about various films in which people were impaled. He began to talk about the film "Armageddon" and about an asteroid that had hit Paris. After a while, when I mentioned that these were sad stories he was telling me, he talked for a moment about how many people were dying of AIDS every day; but then he immediately brought his phallic-narcissistic defences back to the fore and returned to indulging in destructive fantasies. They allowed him to ward off a fleeting perception of his feelings of deep depression with its related anxieties. He had, however, at least been able to pick up this side of his inner experience briefly when I addressed it.

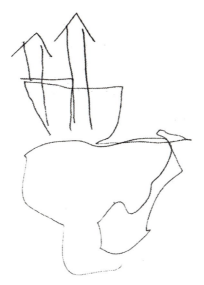

Fig. 4–7: Johannes, Old Celtic castle

He turned my next squiggle into a drop of water (fig. 4–8) that was falling down. However, his phallic-destructive side immediately regained the upper hand, and he scribbled around wildly on the next sheet of paper. He had done that intentionally, he said, so I would always have something difficult to deal with—then, without even drawing breath, he continued: "When's it time for lunch? I'm starved! Why don't you make a Viking ship? What's their heaven called again? Teutoburg is an old castle like that too." I did indeed follow his suggestion, and drew a kind of Viking ship (fig. 4–9), but more or less without any connection to his squiggle, feeling left behind and somewhat puzzled by his hectic activity. Next he drew a time bomb (fig. 4–10). He was drawing and talking about nothing but dangerous things, I said inquiringly. "Massacre is my hobby. On the computer you have to fight each other, there are massive battles with cavalry. My friend's worse than I am," Johannes explained to me. We went on to talk a bit more about massacres, and finally he said that it wasn't just massacres; it was strategy too. You had to feed your own people as well. So you have to watch out, I said, that you don't get massacred yourself. Johannes said: "Hmm. Now this is a bomb." With his next squiggle he suggested that I could make a nut or an almond out of it, or an egg. I made an acorn (fig. 4–11). Next

Fig. 4–8: Johannes, Drop of water, falling

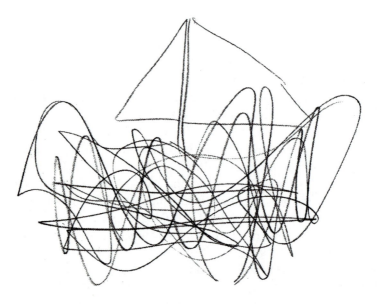

Fig. 4–9: Johannes, Viking ship

he drew a *Gummibär* [a bear-shaped jelly sweet, manufactured by Haribo] (fig. 4–12) and referred to the Haribo advert [in which a famous chat-show host talks to them and then eats them all up]. You had to watch out that no one ran over them and no one ate them, he said. Then he needed to go to the toilet very urgently.

Fig. 4–10: Johannes, Time bomb

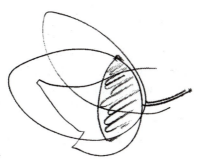

Fig. 4–11: Johannes, Acorn

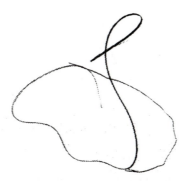

Fig. 4–12: Johannes, *Gummibärchen* (jelly bear)

The soft sides that were still quite undefined in the first part of the interview became selectively a little firmer in the second part, and I understood them as a deep desire for dependence and loving care at an oral level. If we could free the nut or almond of its hard shell, or remove the egg-shell, a jelly-bear would emerge, in extreme danger from the projected aggressive-destructive sides, but also from the refusal of the environment (Winnicott) even to see or take note of these other sides. In retrospect, therefore, the acorn I had drawn could also be regarded as an attempt to bring together hard and soft, shell and kernel, phallic potency and the threat to it. I was very moved by the interview with Johannes, because despite his unsettled, erratic, sometimes pushy and overbearing manner, always trying to maintain control over what was going on, he had made it clear at various points in the course of the interview, in his drawings and the commentaries on them, that he had another hidden side. I understood these signals on his part as hesitant attempts to ask whether there might not be some hope for him here at the hospital, that these sides would be discovered and he would not be defined only by his bad and nasty behaviour. It was clear to me that his question was also whether there could be a containing frame for the aggressive and destructive sides of himself that ran through the whole conversation in the pictures, as well as a protective frame for the endangered sides of his true self, as conveyed in the last picture. As I saw it, the almost shapeless form of the jelly-bear corresponded to a soft, still undeveloped childlike part of his self, and we had to create a space for it, not least to shield it from his own aggressive-destructive defence.

Given this understanding, I was not surprised to find out afterwards that Johannes had repeatedly contemplated suicide. He had, among other things, thought of slitting his wrists; and had on one previous occasion also tied a rope with a hangman's noose to a beam and considered hanging himself.

The squiggle interview gave me the means of conveying in a very vivid form something of the boy's two sides to my colleagues on the ward. At the beginning of his in-patient treatment, he could only allow himself to show his soft, vulnerable sides, which also contained something like a grain of hope, for brief moments, and almost exclusively in a protected situation such as an individual therapy interview, while on the ward he behaved in the usual aggressive, antisocial manner. However, through intensive discussions, and with the help of this squiggle interview among other things, the staff on the ward were able to get an idea of this boy's desperate inner need, and they were increasingly able to maintain this image of Johannes' other side even in difficult situations with him. In this way they were able to prevent themselves from becoming captives of his negative identity, his outrageous behaviour and his impulsive aggressive outbursts to an extent that would have undermined his treatment.

During his subsequent nine-month in-patient treatment, Johannes gradually became able to give up his antisocial and aggressive-destructive behaviour, and he was increasingly able to cope with disappointment. He was also able to find better ways of resolving difficult situations in everyday life with other children, so that at the end of the treatment he was much more stable and could deal in a very different way with internal processes of disappointment and sadness, with loss anxieties and the feeling of not being loved.

In the course of Johannes' treatment, we learned a great deal about the traumatic background which had led to such a difficult situation. His parents had already broken up once when his mother was pregnant with him, and had considered aborting the child. Having got back together, the parents separated again when he was two. From early infancy Johannes had cried often and persistently, and had been hard to calm down; this suggested stress in the relationship on the one hand, and disturbance in the regulation of affects and sleep on the other hand. When he started at kindergarten, he developed separation anxieties, conspicuously obstinate and aggressive behaviour and increased hyperactivity. It may be that the image of a difficult child who disappoints his mother and is disappointed by her had taken hold early on in the mutual interaction between mother and child.

The relationship with his natural father had suffered as well, due to the parents' separation and later the ending of visits; his mother also told us that his father was unreliable. The stepfather had taken an interest in him at first, but this gave way to indifference and resignation. The stepfather also hit the boy quite frequently, so that the whole situation became even more acute, both internally and externally, with the arrival of two half-siblings, born when Johannes was seven and nine. In his eyes—and also in reality—they were favoured by the parents. The mother had become highly ambivalent towards her son, whereas the stepfather was unequivocal in his rejection of him, although he said that his heavy workload also played a part in this.

When it became clear that the stepfather in particular could not envisage providing anything like the high degree of paternal presence that would obviously be needed when Johannes returned home, we reached an understanding with the parents a few months before his actual discharge from in-patient treatment that Johannes should not return home, but should be placed in a residential home. This decision caused him deep distress when he was told, and he became suicidal again as a result, especially because his parents told him at the same time that his mother had considered aborting him. During the period that followed, it was rough going for Johannes and for us to work through the related anxieties and affects of anger, as well as his sadness. In the process, Johannes became increasingly able to deal with these conflicts internally and in the therapy sessions, and resorted less frequently to the relief function of aggressive-destructive behaviour on the ward. As far as we know, Johannes has now settled into the residential home and visits his parents regularly during the weekend.

Children and adolescents with antisocial development pose a real challenge in psychotherapy sessions, especially if a negative identity has already taken hold. These children have to protect themselves subjectively, have to be wary of any offer to form a relationship with them, as this in their eyes inevitably becomes a trap from the moment they start to place their trust in it. All too often their experience is that every new relationship, every new attempt to give someone the benefit of the doubt has ended in disappointment. The fact that this is partly their own doing, that with their mistrust of every deeper emotional tie and with the destructiveness of their defences, they themselves repeatedly contribute significantly to creating the situation, is initially fairly irrelevant if we want to make contact with these children. The squiggle game often allows me to establish an initial contact, especially in the case of younger adolescents and older children with antisocial development.

These children do not always open up as quickly as Johannes, who conveyed the drama of his existence with a striking image in his very first picture. In many cases, defences, obstinate refusal and aggressive rejection prevail at first, but usually the children are at least willing to convey feelings such as these in the squiggle game. A child may at first continuously scribble all over the sheets of paper, try to make things as difficult as possible for the therapist, or make no attempt whatsoever to do anything with the therapist's squiggle. However, if we address this refusal, in most cases it will in fact usually lead to a dialogue, as soon as the child has the feeling that his other softer, hidden side is being addressed and recognized. But caution will often develop to the same degree as trust begins to emerge. These children quickly withdraw again after opening up for a moment, and are usually not able to develop a theme continuously over the course of several pictures if it touches them inwardly and would make them vulnerable. It is the therapist's task to capture some of this, as if in a snapshot, even if there is no opportunity to go into it more deeply in the subsequent conversation. I am nonetheless convinced that these children, who are so disturbed in their capacity to relate to others and yet so sensitive to every nuance of the relationship, do indeed register the one moment when genuine contact was made and hold on to it for themselves. At the same time, they pay very close attention to whether their barrier, their form of antisocial and manipulative defence against anxiety, is being undermined by manipulative counter-manoeuvres, or is being respected for once. In this respect, the fleeting nature of the squiggle game, jumping from one picture to another, works with these children and can yield a good start. The work from there on, however, still remains an arduous and often also risky undertaking for child and therapist alike.

CHAPTER FIVE

Deep impact: "They are all nutcases"

Martin, aged 13

M artin had twice been brought in to us in an ambulance after threatening his mother. The first time it was reported that he had initially pestered his mother because he wanted to buy some things. During the car journey he had smashed the rear view mirror and damaged the dashboard. Back at home, he had taken the family phone to his room and locked himself in. The mother had complained about telephone bills amounting to hundreds of euros. In the end he had smashed the phone. On a number of occasions he had threatened her with a knife. The mother also reported that she herself had needed admission to hospital for psychotherapeutic treatment because of the stress the boy had caused her. Martin had been placed in a residential home at that time, but she had taken him back home after massive pressure, in actual fact after threats (which were not detailed) from him. Before this period in the residential home, Martin had already been admitted for child psychiatric treatment at the age of nine. He had threatened to kill his mother and himself. There were repeated aggressive outbursts at home, during which he would destroy objects. He had already injured his mother and used abusive language to her. He completely lost control if his mother scolded him.

On the night when 13-year-old Martin was brought in by ambulance, he seemed at first completely unexceptional in his behaviour. He had calmed down completely, and reported in a disciplined and quite realistic manner on the situation at home. After his mother appeared a little later, the picture changed perceptibly. A highly tense and ambivalence-laden conflict situation developed between mother and child in which both became verbally aggressive, but on the other hand considerable fears also became apparent on both sides. Martin became emotionally unstable and oscillated between aggressive phantasies, self-accusations, moments of desperation and markedly theatrical behaviour with which he exerted pressure on his mother. For her part, the mother reported that she had always experienced the son, like his father, as very dominant. Martin had been born out of wedlock. Since his third year there had been no contact for many years, but now the father was tyrannizing her. Sure enough, in the middle of this highly charged situation during the emergency admission, the father happened to ring the son on his mobile phone, and told me straight away that in his opinion the son was perfectly normal, it was just the mother who was mad. On Martin's and his mother's urging I discharged him that same night. A few days later he was brought in again, arriving by ambulance with a police escort. He had lost control of himself at home, and after he had left to go to school, his mother had called the police. Again I admitted him as an emergency to our children's ward.

The next day I suggested that we should try a squiggle interview. He first drew a joystick (fig. 5–1) and told me that he enjoyed playing computer games. With my first picture (fig. 5–2), which depicted a duck, I seemed to make contact with a very childlike, emotionally retarded side of him: he thought the duck was sweet. His next drawing was an armchair (fig. 5–3). You could sink right down in it, it was like my armchair, a really relaxing chair to snuggle into, he said. That's what he liked doing on the sofa at home. There was in fact an armchair like that in my consulting room, and I was sitting in it during the interview. Martin was clearly making contact with me on the level of his childlike need for closeness. I imagine that one factor in this was that he had experienced me twice now in situations which were difficult for him and his mother, and on both occasions I had made the option of in-patient admission available more as an offer of protection than as a measure intended to set limits. I turned his next squiggle into a man on a motorbike (fig. 5–4), presumably identifying with the fact that there were other sides to

Fig. 5–1: Martin, Joystick

Fig. 5–2: Martin, Duck

him. He responded with an enormous wave (fig. 5–5). It reminded him of the film "Deep impact", in which a comet hit the Earth and caused a huge wave to inundate New York. I said: "That is a real catastrophe." Martin responded: "Yes, if you imagine all the people." So we had arrived at the real central theme.

In the next picture I simply added a television set to his squiggle, remarking that his squiggle also resembled a comfortable armchair

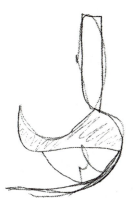

Fig. 5–3: Martin, Armchair

Fig. 5–4: Martin, Man on a motorbike

Fig. 5–5: Martin, Enormous wave

Fig. 5–6: Martin, Comfortable chair and television set

(fig. 5–6). It reminded him of a mother bending down to pick up her baby, he said spontaneously. I drew his attention to the difference between this and the previous picture. Martin said: "Yes, the wave is threatening, and the mother . . . well, she protects."

He made a waffle iron out of the next scribble (fig. 5–7). They couldn't make waffles at home at the moment because the waffle iron was broken. He only ate pizza anyway, he said. After school he was always so done in that he came home and got really furious and

Fig. 5–7: Martin, Waffle iron

shouted at his mother. Then it was stupid and his mother was fed up. So he developed his theme logically and consistently: his mother didn't satisfy his desire to be looked after—the waffle iron was broken. He would get angry about this and they would have a fight. I interpreted this connection to him and said it would be nice to be little again. He agreed, but said it was a bit difficult as he was in a higher class at school; his marks had gone down quite a bit. When I led him back to the theme of his desire for loving care at an oral level, he was able to speak about the conflict between the childlike desire to be looked after by his mother and the early adolescent striving to break away by orientating himself to his mates and the clique.

My next drawing was a frog (fig. 5–8), and Martin felt he had to reassure me that I didn't have to worry that it was hard to make out, my drawings were real works of art. I thought to myself that this was probably something he had to do with his parents, to stabilize their narcissistic balance, but I said no more about it. He promptly started his next picture with the comment that it was difficult, but he managed to make an ice cream van out of it (fig. 5–9) which, I would say, assured his oral satisfaction. This van was driving up the hill. (They did in fact live on a hill.) His mother had just ordered

Fig. 5–8: Martin, Frog

Fig. 5–9: Martin, Ice cream van

ice cream and this van was driving up the hill to them. We agreed that we were back with our theme. A very clear and understandable pattern of reactions was presenting itself here: narcissistic stabilization of the parents was followed by provision for his own oral needs. With my next picture, which represented a woman seen from behind (fig. 5–10), the process swung back again, and he assured me that

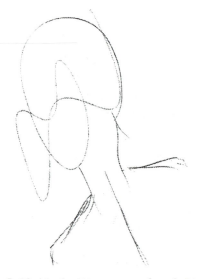

Fig. 5–10: Martin, Woman seen from behind

Fig. 5–11: Martin, Woman with messy hair, Pokémon

the picture looked good. He took up my motif and drew a woman himself (fig. 5–11), saying that this was a woman with messy hair from Pokémon. She and someone else wanted to dominate the whole world and kidnap Pikachu, a very small Pokémon. They were always joking around and fighting all the time. They were all nutcases. She had red, wavy hair and was called Jessy. I think at this stage Martin was referring to the madness of his parents, who were not able to guarantee little Pikachu the protection and stability he needed. Indeed, as we discovered, the father was an alcoholic, was always verbally destructive, and had become aggressive and violent. Martin told us a few days later that he was quite a show-off, shouting at his employees and playing around with weapons, and that he worked when he felt like it. His mother also used to drink.

I made a rubber stamp out of his next squiggle (fig. 5–12). He commented instantly: "You bang on that." He would have thought the scribble was a man sitting cross-legged, praying. There were some who developed powers in praying and began to float. They escaped the force of gravity and heard their inner voice. If it began to crackle, they'd suddenly fall back down. If he was like that, he wouldn't have to be here. Then he'd be a master and would teach children, but

Fig. 5–12: Martin, Rubber stamp

because he got so worked up this wasn't possible. I felt that this was a distinctly creative and imaginative, if not really feasible, solution for his difficulties.

He drew a fish (fig. 5–13). When I pointed out the big mouth, which he had made very conspicuous, he said that was good, it could eat a lot. Otherwise it would starve and die if it didn't get enough to eat. The next picture I drew was an iron (fig. 5–14), which I think continued the theme of domestic care. In his last picture he drew a bottle of rum (fig. 5–15), and when I interpreted the little heart-shaped figure next to it as a drunken fly, he corrected me. No, this was a rum bottle with a ribbon on it, and at the end of the ribbon was a heart. This was rum for peace and freedom. It would be a present for his mother, although she didn't drink alcohol but she could put the bottle up somewhere if it was fluorescent blue. (His actual words could have referred on the one hand consciously to the bottle or on the other hand unconsciously to his mother as "going blue", i.e. getting drunk.) I asked him at this point if his mother had ever drunk in the past, which was something I didn't know then, and he said yes. That had been bad, but now she just smoked, fortunately. But he was sometimes afraid she'd get cancer. I told him that I could now understand why he had refused to stay at the clinic

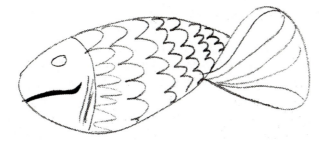

Fig. 5–13: Martin, Fish

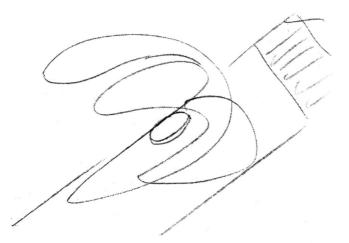

Fig. 5–14: Martin, Iron

Fig. 5–15: Martin, Bottle of rum with ribbon and heart

or to take up our suggestion of going to a residential home for young people: it was because he had been anxious about his mother and had to look after her. At this he became very thoughtful and confirmed my suspicion. When we looked back over the pictures, he said he had to add something to the joystick to make sure it held.

On the same day, Martin talked to his therapist on the ward and told him that saying goodbye to the residential home then had been very hard for him. In particular he had very much liked going to school there and still missed his favourite teacher. He would really like to go back to this previous home. A few days later we were able to let Martin go home temporarily, after arranging for him to be taken back in to his previous residential home.

Martin had in earlier treatments been regarded and diagnosed as having ADHD with hyperactivity. It is true that his behaviour showed signs of hyperactivity, lack of appropriate distance and impulsiveness. On closer inspection, a more differentiated picture emerged. The symptoms were a reaction to and expression of a dramatic inner situation which had intensified over many years of exposure to constantly changing unstable outer relationships. This is not to say that the parents, both the mother and the father, did not in their own way look after the boy and try, as far as they were able, to stabilize the situation. However, both of them suffered from dramatic deficits of their own, so that Martin was trapped in multiple relational dilemmas. On the one hand it was up to him to stabilize the narcissistic problems of his parents; on the other hand he identified with the corresponding narcissistic omnipotence fantasies which, above all on the father's side, also took on violent and destructive forms. Thus in identifying with the father and with unconscious inner objects of the mother, he became a child who battered his mother. In a mutual, secret collusion which was nevertheless marked by desperation, a battered parents syndrome developed. He also suffered from the insufficient satisfaction of his childlike needs. This, like the aggressive-destructive identifications, contributed to his intense fear of separation, yet simultaneously drove his aggressive-destructive behaviour.

In such cases, it is only when attention is given to the actual dynamics of the inner conflict in a child that the hidden, softer sides and the need for affection and attachment can be discovered and addressed. This succeeded surprisingly well with Martin, because his antisocial defences were evidently not so firmly cemented as to make it extremely difficult to reach the layers beneath. In this respect, a squiggle interview in which an understanding is reached with the child can offer an insight into the dynamics of his inner conflicts. At the same time, if the antisocial defence structures are not yet hardened, such a conversation can also trigger a change of mood which, as in Martin's case, can bring about an opening and give the child new confidence. If this succeeds, a fresh start is possible. The subsequent work will be hard enough, because the more confidence the child gains, the more he will begin to put a strain on the newly-won relationships and therefore feel great anxiety about fresh disappointment. Often the only way he can defend himself against this fear is by attacking the basis of the relationship.

For this reason, a successful squiggle interview with such children can in some ways turn out to be double-edged. It offers a promise which has yet to be redeemed. In making the child feel understood, the interview tempts him into entertaining fresh hope. Yet without such an experience of being understood, which may sometimes also emerge in a good pedagogical relationship, the child's only available course is to adopt antisocial behaviour.

CHAPTER SIX

A lion and a broken comb: problematic identification with the father after a traumatic previous history

Samir, aged 7

S amir, aged seven years and nine months, comes from Chechnya, from where the family had fled a year before. Not long before they left for Germany, he spent three months as an in-patient in a children's neuropsychiatric clinic, where he was diagnosed with progressive autism. In Germany, Samir had been admitted to the child neurology ward for further clarification of his case. I was called in by colleagues to determine whether this was indeed a case of autism or whether he was suffering from some other severe psychiatric illness, and what further measures could be useful from the point of view of child psychiatry.

Samir meanwhile spoke a little German, so that he could at least make himself understood. The interpreter who attended the interview was able to limit herself to translating single words that he didn't know. In fact I had to speak to him in very simple terms not only because he understood and spoke very limited German, but also because his intellectual abilities were clearly limited, that is to say he had a severe learning impediment.

First of all I spoke to Samir. Initially he refused even to come with me to another room, but then agreed to do so if his mother was allowed to be present at the interview as well as the interpreter. I allowed this. Samir was quite restless throughout our conversation and also unable to keep an appropriate distance. He had difficulty keeping to the framework that I gave him. He kept wanting to stop, run away, or do something else. It was quite an effort to keep his concentration.

In our subsequent conversation, the mother told us essentially that Samir had always been isolated. He was teased and excluded by his peers. His impulsiveness and hyperactive behaviour irritated people everywhere, both at school and in the afternoons when he was with other children. He was afraid of other children, she said. By contrast his twin brother was socially integrated and well liked by his peers. The twin brother was doing well at a mainstream school whereas Samir went to a special school.

As to his early history, we knew from the short report given by the child neuropsychiatry department in Chechnya that Samir was born by Caesarean section and that during his mother's pregnancy and his early development no problems had arisen. The report described occasional seizures, the first time during a rocket attack, a second time as a result of food poisoning after eating a watermelon. He had been given anti-epileptic treatment. Now, in our hospital, doubt was expressed by the neurologists as to his being prone to seizures, as they had seen no evidence of this in the time he had spent here. At the time of his treatment in the child neuropsychiatric clinic, both the disturbance in his ability to make contact and his restlessness had already been noticed. There had been moments of "freezing" which were interpreted as catatonic symptoms. He had sometimes put on strange voices, remembered war heroes from cartoon films, and walked round in circles. This general state had, however, improved during his stay.

A squiggle interview seemed to me to offer the best possibility of making contact with him. He drew a giraffe out of my first squiggle (fig. 6–1)—to be more precise, a giraffe's head, and we talked a little about giraffes, mainly about how high up in the air their heads were. He switched very soon to talking about lions. Instead of making a squiggle he drew a lion (fig. 6–2), finishing off by drawing a huge mane around its head. He then added a tiger and talked about how the lion would beat the tiger. The lion was much stronger than the tiger. Samir thus moved straight away into narcissistic phantasies of omnipotence with shades of aggression. This contrasted with his drawing skills, which were not quite what would be expected at his age. Out of my next squiggle he made a broken comb (fig. 6–3). His father had broken it when he stood on it. Then Samir said the comb

Fig. 6–1: Samir, Giraffe head

Fig. 6–2: Samir, Lion with a huge mane

Fig. 6–3: Samir, Broken comb

had simply got broken. Following on from this he became very restless, and his behaviour seemed disorganized and chaotic. I found it very striking here that he placed phantasies of omnipotence directly next to the breaking of things, and had the impression that these two types of experience had imprinted themselves on his perception.

The next step was that Samir again drew a whole picture, not a squiggle (fig. 6–4). This was a boy who hit, who ran away and who went to school. In the school there was a toilet. Next he tried to write the name of the boy, Berry. He did indeed begin with the letter B, but then continued with the letters of his own name. He thereby made it clear to me that in talking about Berry he was talking about himself, summing up his experience of himself nearly as starkly as in a woodcut: boy hits others; boy is afraid and runs away; boy goes to school. Thus he himself named the three biggest problem areas, which had also been named by his mother. From my next scribble he made a pair of glasses (fig. 6–5). The glasses are broken, he commented. Afterwards he wasn't sure whether they were really glasses or goggles. Again he referred to something being broken, which confirmed that this was something central in his experience. Rather speculatively at this point, of course, we might connect this with the experience that what he did always led to destruction, with the experience that things and relationships which were important to him got broken, with his experience of war in Grozny, or, as he had hinted earlier, a problematic, as it were "broken" identification

Fig. 6–4: Samir, Boy who hits, runs away and goes to school

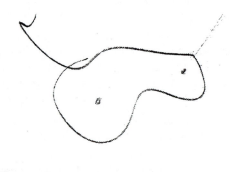

Fig. 6–5: Samir, Broken glasses

with his father. Connections such as these could be kept in the back of our mind as a working hypothesis to be tested in longer-term psychotherapy, but they could not be verified with the material available in this session.

Once again he drew his own picture, not a squiggle: this time a figure (fig. 6–6). This was Bruce Lee, he said, or rather Michael Jackson; in the end it was Superman. He has a cape, he said, and added a cape. He also had a ring on his chest which was attached to a chain. At this point I commented that he had drawn such a lot of fantastic animals and people, first the lion and now Superman and Bruce Lee and Michael Jackson. Perhaps he would like to be fantastic too. He became very animated at this intervention and said with utter conviction that he could do anything Superman could do. But the next moment this mood collapsed and he said he couldn't even write

Fig. 6–6: Samir, Bruce Lee or Michael Jackson or Superman

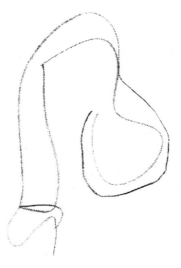

Fig. 6–7: Samir, Giraffe

and was tired. Then a moment later he was sliding off into phantasies of omnipotence again. Finally he added a bank robber or a witch at the top of the page. The witch was setting fire to something. In the end he jumped back to Superman, who could fly. It was more than clear to me how unstable his identifications were, how rapidly he leapt from one to the next, and how close to each other were his phantasies of omnipotence, his aggressive phantasies and his fear that everything would be destroyed.

For his last picture he drew another giraffe (fig. 6–7). This now was a big giraffe, the first had been the baby. I commented here that this one could also be the other giraffe's twin. No, he said, this was the big giraffe and the other one was the baby. He said he didn't want to be a twin and that he had no twin brother. Looking back on this, I am convinced that in this final drawing he was addressing his position as a twin. This obviously preoccupied and hurt him so deeply that he had to deny having a twin brother who was so much more successful both socially and at school. When I made this explicit, the subject clearly seemed too difficult for him and he didn't want to speak to me about it any further at that point in the interview.

It would have made no sense to try and conduct such an interview verbally, given Samir's symptoms and language problems. We could of course have observed his behaviour, but would certainly not have been able to gain an insight into his inner world and conflicts. Using the squiggle game it was possible to find out far more about this inner world, about his narcissistic phantasies of omnipotence and also about the destruction of inner objects. Alongside the child psychiatrist's diagnosis of a hyperkinetic disturbance of social behaviour with social withdrawal and aggressiveness, I was able to form a first impression of what was preoccupying him internally and making him so difficult in his behaviour.

I would like to make it quite clear that I am not concerned here with discussing the aetiology of the illness. In the case of this boy there will certainly have been a close and dynamic interaction between neuropsychological impairments and stressful experiences in relationships, so that we should take as our starting point a psychosomatic or somatopsychic complementary series. In fact the development of many children who suffer from attention deficit disorder will depend largely on what kind of relationship experiences they have been able to internalize and how unstable their internal psychic structure is. As to the aetiology of this syndrome in detail, however detailed our understanding of it may be, as research continues, the situation will certainly turn out to be even more complex than we can begin to guess.

With Samir, we saw that the accumulated stresses had led outwardly to severe impairment in his development and inwardly to an unstable structure with narcissistic phantasies of omnipotence on the one hand and a problematic fixation on destroyed inner objects on the other. Naturally we would treat the insights gained in such an interview as well-founded working hypotheses which could at least make clear how important it would be for Samir that work be done on stabilizing outer structures, but above all on stabilizing his inner object worlds.

Samir's mother mainly sat quietly to one side during the interview, but I spoke to her again afterwards and explained what I thought I had seen. Above all I commented to her that I felt he compared himself to a great extent with his brother and that this unfavourable comparison posed a considerable problem for him. His mother confirmed that he suffered a great deal over this. I recommended out-patient treatment adapted to his intellectual level, and was able to demonstrate the importance of this using the pictures he drew in the interview. Alongside this treatment I suggested trying methyl-phenidate, primarily to achieve a little relief in terms of his derailed social relationships. If this succeeds, such relief can help the child to experience himself differently and to be experienced differently in his social relationships.

Many questions still remained open in Samir's case. Interviews of this type in particular will reveal how strikingly inner dynamics can come to light, but also how much more patient further work is needed to make sure our ideas are correct, to determine more precisely how the dynamics are connected, and above all to treat the intense inner conflicts. One element that was completely missing in this case was the father. In the interview there were moments that pointed to him: the breaking of the comb, the school building with toilet (whatever these may have meant to the boy in concrete terms) or the depiction of heroes in the sixth picture. It was easy to see that there were problems with regard to identification with the father and internalization of a stable fatherly example. The interview did not, however, provide enough information (for me at least) to describe the related conflicts in detail, or to determine what specific contents were connected to this theme.

CHAPTER SEVEN

The oh-so-good angel and the sock

Elisa, aged 10

E lisa, aged ten years and nine months, was admitted to the clinic for child and adolescent psychiatry because she was suffering from severe encopresis. She had soiled herself several times a day since early childhood with one doubtful interruption of six months, withdrew from social contact, and barely spoke to people outside the family. Since the age of three or four she had received occasional therapy because she displayed general developmental delay. At school and with her peers, on the one hand she was an outsider and was teased (among other names she was called Stink-bomb); on the other hand she often allowed her schoolmates to harass her sexually without being able to set any limits to it. Sometimes she triggered these encounters herself. Staff at the day care group she attended described her as scruffy and neglected. She was finally excluded from the centre and was about to be expelled from school.

On first impression the girl seemed to be mentally retarded not only in her appearance but also in her behaviour. She initially made virtually no verbal contact, after admission to the children's ward she behaved increasingly like a three-year-old, and if she spoke to us at all, she communicated exclusively in one- or two-word sentences. Her linguistic repertoire in vocabulary and intonation was taken almost exclusively from "Teletubbies", a television programme

This chapter is a revised version of Günter, 2000

for toddlers. She spoke like the Teletubbies, behaved like a Teletubby, and seemed to live in this harmonious toddler phantasy world. As regards her symptoms, she showed no sign of motivation to change and consistently refused to go to the toilet to pass stools.

After Elisa had been on the ward for a few weeks and we had established an initial contact with her at least in Teletubby conversations, we suggested to her that we could use laxative suppositories to regulate her stools. However, she developed intense fears, falling into an acute state of anxious excitation with dissociation when the first suppository was given to her. It was the awareness of body processes after she was given the suppository that triggered an intense fear affect. She expressed a fear that she would not be able to stop passing stool when she was on the toilet. While she had previously said that she was afraid it would hurt when she passed stool, now the real deprivation and related deeper levels of pathological organisation could be approached. She said spontaneously: "If I don't soil my pants my mother won't do anything with me any more. My mother doesn't like me any more. She just looks after my sister all the time. There's something else bad with my father. But I can't say that now or I'll never be allowed to go back home." In this situation we had to stop giving her any more suppositories for the time being, until our contact with her and her confidence in us were more stable.

In this way a specific medical intervention enabled us for the first time to access her intense depressive and paranoid fears. However, a lengthy and very difficult process of therapy was required to make these fears more accessible in the therapeutic relationship, to work on them and to be able to understand their actual background better. Gradually she became a little more open in school and in the children's group, and gained a little self-confidence. By contrast, her therapist described her as remaining very reserved and uncommunicative in therapy sessions, particularly if he addressed any presumed conflicts.

Along with coaching in school work, Elisa's treatment centred mainly on personal hygiene. Our discussions in connection with this were on the one hand aimed at supporting Elisa in learning to look after herself to an extent appropriate to her age, something she had never had the chance to learn at home as a result of her deprived circumstances. On the other hand, this intensive attention devoted to her body was part of our therapeutic offer of a relationship, designed to enable her to leave the narcissistic cocoon formed of stink and pseudo-feeble-mindedness in favour of allowing herself to be involved in relationships which were initially fraught with fears to an extreme degree.

At the same time the therapist treating Elisa tried to work with her on what manifold regulatory functions the holding back of faeces, the refusal to go to the toilet, the constant soiling and the associated stink might have for her. This entrenched behaviour maintained the omnipotent phantasy of a symbiotic relationship to the mother with no need for separation. It also represented a barrier against the fears of persecution in the course of which the entire outer world was experienced as threatening and persecuting. Her pseudo-feeble-minded withdrawal from the world worked in the same direction, as did her inability to learn, which often made the therapeutic sessions immensely difficult. She withdrew every time anyone tried to address the dynamics between her regressive withdrawal into an omnipotent-infantile world and her defiant refusal.

It was a good six months after her admission to the ward that the following squiggle interview with Elisa took place. From my first scribble she drew something she called a perfumer (fig. 7–1). We

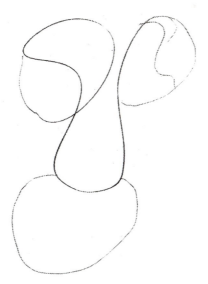

Fig. 7–1: Elisa, Perfumer

agreed that the bottle was at the bottom and at the top were two "sort of perfume parts". Thus she was making a direct reference to her symptoms straight away and formulating a wish to overcome the stink. Her own squiggle made her think of something straight away and I encouraged her to draw it. She drew Teletubbyland (fig. 7–2) and the Teletubbies with their attributes. She didn't want to tell me a story about them at first, but afterwards volunteered that she liked the Teletubbies. Finally she told me she had once seen a programme in which the Teletubbies' toys grew larger and larger. Dipsy, one of the Teletubbies, had not been able to see anything, the toys had grown so big. With this story she conveyed her regressive wish to be so small that the toys would seem big again. She then finished the story logically, with an infantile oral satisfaction: the Teletubbies always ate Tubby custard and Tubby toast. That was their favourite food.

Out of my next squiggle she drew a person (fig. 7–3). This was a grown-up, she said. In view of the last picture and of Elisa's deprived background, and also because of the figure's large tummy, I suggested that it looked like a Mummy. No, she said, it looked more

Fig. 7–2: Elisa, Teletubbyland

like a man. The man was just looking where his ball had gone, because he was playing golf. The ball would certainly fly into the hole. This remark made me wonder, particularly as I had also suddenly noticed the lines sticking out from his belly, whether it might be an indication of sexual attacks. But I waited without saying anything, and made a person playing a concertina out of her next squiggle (fig. 7–4).

From my next squiggle she very rapidly drew a figure (fig. 7–5) and said "That is an angel . . . he's just dropping a leaf or something . . . there's a flower on it . . . onto the ground . . . and then a child finds it and shows it to his mother, maybe gives it to her as a present . . . mother and child are happy with it." I pointed out that the arms and legs were missing. They were hidden in the robe, Elisa said. Thereupon I asked her if she would like to be small again. She became restless and replied evasively that she didn't know. When I rather insistently asked again, she said Mummy was happy because she was always so good. She remained very restless and made it clear that she did not want to carry on talking about this. I made a cup out of her next scribble (fig. 7–6), and Elisa said there should be cocoa in it, hot and with sugar. From my next she drew "a child eating" (fig. 7–7). She added a fork. The child was eating noodles and sauce.

Fig. 7–3: Elisa, Person

Fig. 7–4: Elisa, Concertina player

Fig. 7–5: Elisa, Angel dropping a leaf

Fig. 7–6: Elisa, Cup

Fig. 7–7: Elisa, A child eating

So we were staying with the childlike needs for loving care at an oral level and for an unbroken relationship with the mother.

From her next squiggle I drew a big sack (fig. 7–8). Without hesitating, she said spontaneously that she would have made a duck out of it, or a child. My scribble was the child's dress. I picked up her comment and said yes, that was a princess's dress, and made a connection to the first picture by saying that she might like to be a sweet-smelling princess. Then she made my next squiggle into a child

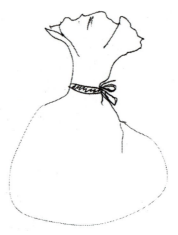

Fig. 7–8: Elisa, Big sack

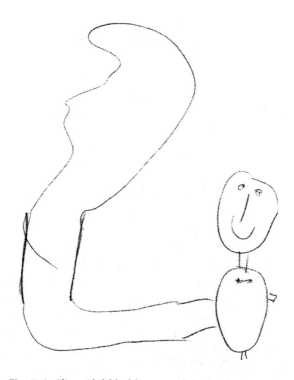

Fig. 7–9: Elisa, Child holding a sock he is playing with

holding a sock that he was playing with (fig. 7–9). This sock was talking to the other socks, asking how things were. I fell in with the sock conversation, holding up my hand as if it were covered in a speaking sock. With this fictitious talking sock I asked her how things were. She replied "Fine". Things would be fine with me, I interpreted her inner situation speaking through my sock-hand, if I were a little child like the Teletubbies (at this she laughed) or if I were a really lovely princess with a cloud of perfume and a dress. Elisa's voice changed; she suddenly felt visibly uncomfortable and said she wanted to play something else. I did not let go at this point but persisted with the topic and asked her again. She agreed that things would be better if she were a small child or a princess. She was now able to speak about how nice it would be to put on a beautiful dress. She sighed and said "If one smells nicer". Or if one put on pretty shoes. At this point she turned down my suggestion that each of us could draw one last picture. She suggested instead that she would like us to play with the doll's house together. She occupied herself in the last five minutes of the session with the toilet from the toy box, which was the first thing she placed in the doll's house. Finally, at the end of our session, she put the monkey on the toilet seat.

There were, of course, many layers to the references in this interview. I picked out above all the aspect of narcissistic and regressive withdrawal which finally allowed Elisa to address her desire for contact and development. In this phase of her treatment it was becoming clearer that in addition to any other deprivation, the child had been abused by her father in that he had watched sex videos with her in the marital bed. As far as we knew he had not carried out any direct sexual activities with her. This other dimension of mistreatment, the sexual abuse, was also mirrored in the interview. We only have to think of the first picture, which from this perspective looks like a penis with testicles and a semen stain, or the picture of the princess (angel) who is dropping a flower and has no hands or feet. I had not been given this very new information at the time of the interview, and even if I had, I would probably not have spoken to the girl about it directly. Elisa had shared with me something of her desperate search for a way out of her negative identity and out of the narcissistic cocoon she had spun around herself. If I had mentioned this aspect of her traumatic reality to her then, not only would it probably have been too much for her, but with such a reference to the past I would also have missed the chance of her building a relationship with me in the present.

Incidentally, our reaction to this new information was that we talked openly to the parents, to Elisa and to the child protection authorities, and made it clear that she had been wronged and that such a thing was on no account to happen again. After the father had not only admitted the sexual abuse but also apologized to Elisa, we saw further stabilization and opening on her part. Teletubby-talk and behaviour decreased significantly, and Elisa seemed to be developing on all fronts. This welcome improvement did not, however, lead to an end of her encopresis. On the contrary, it intensified until she was soiling herself up to twenty times a day. No change in the symptoms was achieved even through further therapeutic work on a central, now recognisable psychical mechanism whereby she obviously rid herself directly of every kind of feeling, positive or negative, by soiling herself. The team became increasingly desperate and angry, and was developing latent sadistic phantasies, as had already happened in earlier phases of work with her.

In this situation we decided once again to intervene on the symptomatic level. We decided that for a period of 12 days we would give her daily enemas of a mixture of peanut oil and glycerine. This suggestion initially met with bitter opposition from the female attachment figures working with her, who, in view of Elisa's traumatic history, feared that she might be intrusively traumatized again. In the course of a number of discussions, making use among other things of the squiggle drawings, we managed to make it clear that these fears represented countertransference reactions. Using projective identification mechanisms, Elisa had rid herself of paranoid fears by depositing them in the female attachment figures. A perverse sadomasochistic transference relationship had developed in which the aggressive-destructive elements resulted on Elisa's part in her holding on to the symptom and on the team's part in feelings of powerlessness and sadistic phantasies. It was only after unravelling this constellation by analysing the countertransference reactions that we were able to act again.

Seen from the outside, such a process of regaining an ability to act through reflection often leads to a procedure very similar to treatment oriented to medical guidelines or pedagogical principles. Yet it differs fundamentally in its therapeutic effectiveness in that it allows staff and patient a different cathexis of their interaction and thus supports the identifications and processes of change linked to the relationship.

The enemas achieved two things: one was that Elisa was able to talk about wanting to stay little and therefore not wanting to go to the toilet. The radical medical-pedagogical intervention had the effect that this fixation could now be addressed again in the one-to-one therapeutic sessions and so could be worked through. The other effect was that, contrary to earlier fears, Elisa not only took the enemas well but suddenly developed the ability to hold the liquid for the necessary 20 minutes and then go to the toilet and pass stool. We even reached a point where she passed stool, then remained continent and went to the toilet again hours later. What we were particularly pleased about beyond this was that Elisa became far more lively, outgoing and open. She became animated, made jokes, and told us that she was sometimes proud of herself. She began to talk far more. Her autism disappeared almost completely. If we asked her if things were going to stay this way after the twelve days we'd agreed on, she replied with a mischievous smile, "We'll see." She was obviously much relieved by this intervention and no longer suffered to the same extent from her paranoid and depressive fears.

The sock talking to other socks, which was developed by Elisa in this case as her own invention of dialogue, is characteristic of a central point of the squiggle game: it is always a game and at the same time a dialogue between therapist and child. In this respect it does not differ fundamentally from other forms of therapeutic play. The use of puppets in child psychotherapy is a well-known technique to enable the child to express her own wishes, fears and conflicts through the speech of an imaginary third person, a playmate. Like other children through the squiggle game, Elisa was able to approach her secret wishes and to give them expression. She was able to assure herself in this way that they were understood and accepted, and so could finally open up in conversation. However, things cannot be left moving without interruption in a regressive direction; even here, reality demands its tribute: in the end the monkey sits on the toilet. The "two principles of mental functioning" (Freud 1911b) remain in force in the squiggle game, and despite its emphasis on unconscious phantasies, it does not lead to a replacement of the reality principle by the pleasure principle.

CHAPTER EIGHT

The rattlesnake with a knot in its tail

Christian, aged 10

I first met eight-year-old Christian when he was in a urological clinic for treatment and I was called in for consultation. He was suffering from a nonneurogenic neurogenic bladder with hydronephrosis of the right kidney. With Christian, as in other cases of neurogenic bladder dysfunction, chronic urinary dysfunction had led to trabeculation of the bladder and to a build-up of residual urine which was backing up to the kidney, with dilation of the urinary tracts. Because of these serious developments there was a threat of permanent damage to the kidneys with a risk of renal insufficiency. Urological treatment with biofeedback training of the pelvic floor had produced some initial success, but had then had no further effect. It had been necessary to insert a supra-pubic bladder catheter, i.e. to draw off the urine via a tube through the abdominal wall to prevent a build-up of urine and so save the kidneys.

Apart from a primary enuresis, no illness or retardation was reported in Christian's early development. What was noticeable was a very strong bond with his father from an early age. The father had twice been away due to work for three months when Christian was two years old. The present situation was that the parents had separated and divorced eighteen months ago. Christian had asked to stay with his father. Talking to me in the course of the consultant examination during his time at the urology clinic, he said he had sometimes felt that in their quarrels over separation his parents were like a couple of criminals. I perceived him at that time as very anxious on the surface but with quite powerful aggressive phantasies behind this front. He identified very strongly with his father, who was a police officer, and often chose to wear T-shirts that were printed to look like police shirts—as he did at the interview with me. He told me that he often imagined his father as being in tremendous danger, for example in shootings. At the time I recommended that he should as a matter of urgency receive intensive psychotherapy as an out-patient, and if this did not succeed, then admission for in-patient treatment would have to be considered.

A year later, the family presented itself again, this time with the request that we admit Christian as an in-patient. We discovered that the father, who had appeared very co-operative and concerned in our talk earlier, had in fact taken no steps to set up psychotherapy for Christian. In the meantime the kidney problem had intensified, and it was decided that Christian should become an in-patient to receive child psychiatric and psychotherapeutic treatment. During this treatment it became more and more apparent that for years the boy had been emotionally stretched beyond his capacity, depressive and shut off, and he had developed a variety of symptoms from an early age. We could see that the separation of the parents was the last drop that made the cup (here specifically the bladder) run over. We also heard that about a month after I had last seen him, Christian had additionally developed severe encopresis and in the end was soiling himself daily. It might almost be assumed that this symptom appeared after the agreement made with me regarding therapy for him was not kept by his parents. It was not until the kidney situation worsened that the parents, after a bit of back and forth, finally realised that Christian needed in-patient psychotherapeutic treatment.

Christian's symptoms improved rapidly during his in-patient psychotherapeutic treatment and the work on his general psychic disturbance, in particular on the pathological identification with his father, who suffered from a severe anxiety disorder combined with hidden aggression. First of all the boy's migraines disappeared. The daily soiling improved significantly, and disappeared completely in the course of his year-long treatment. The bladder catheter could be removed after three months. The urine retention did not reappear, but in its place there was initially a long period of daytime enuresis, when he was wetting himself up to ten times a day. But that too was significantly reduced by the end of his stay. His eating habits stabilized—he had additionally been suffering from anorexia.

We recommended that Christian should go to a residential home for young people when he left us, but the parents could not agree to this. Despite the fact that their separation was now some time back, the relationship between the parents, though polite on the surface, was in fact characterised by intense quarrels, insults and barely functioning communication. It was only with difficulty that they finally managed to agree that Christian should join his mother after his discharge.

It is not possible here to follow in detail the complex dynamics and treatment history which led the boy step by step to open up and to find relief. It is also not the purpose of this case vignette to illuminate the complex dynamics of his relationships and their manifold identifications in which he had become trapped. I would merely like, against the background of this brief summary of his case history, to report on the squiggle interview that I (as consultant responsible for the ward) carried out with Christian on the day he was discharged after a year spent in the clinic.

After a short conversation on how he was feeling and what his next steps would be, we began our squiggle game. Christian added two little lines to my first squiggle, propped his head on his hand and just sat there (fig. 8–1). Only when I asked him did he say it was

Fig. 8–1: Christian, Foot

a foot. There was a leaf on top, you would have to mentally remove that, he said. I didn't know what to make of this. From his squiggle I made a flower (fig. 8–2). When I quickly identified his next picture (fig. 8–3) as a foot, he denied it indignantly. This was a hand. Normally, he continued, the middle finger is the longest. Again I didn't know what to make of it, and took refuge in a kind of rocking chair that I made out of his next squiggle (fig. 8–4). Hand and foot were too banal, something wasn't right about these body parts.

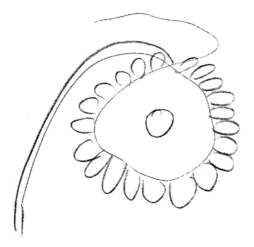

Fig. 8–2: Christian, Flower

Fig. 8–3: Christian, Hand

Fig. 8–4: Christian, Rocking chair

Next he drew a rollercoaster (fig. 8–5). I commented that there were a few people riding on it and wondered (thinking of his present situation) whether they might ride out of it. He commented that the line of the rollercoaster looked like a letter H, you could write HALT there. And then, after a pause he said: "You're not allowed to go any further." He knew people, he said, who could stop cars with a gesture

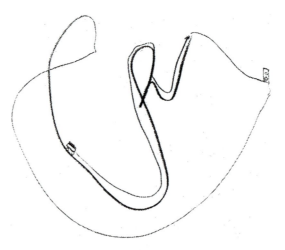

Fig. 8–5: Christian, Rollercoaster

of the hand. I didn't go into the fact that his father was a traffic policeman—in fact it didn't even occur to me that moment. Instead I said HALT made me think of the reason he had come to us. He looked more interested and said "Halt the problems?" So I said: "That the urine wouldn't flow. And originally we thought we could deal with it just having you come in as an out-patient." At this point he mentioned an advert in which it was a question of whether the man had got slower or the world had speeded up. He himself had speeded up. His problem had gone away faster, he said. Then he said he'd forgotten to put something on the picture, and added the ticket office on the right edge. I commented that one had to pay for everything. At this point it seemed clear to me that he was beginning to let himself get involved in the conversation, although his theme only crystallised gradually.

Out of his next squiggle he wanted to make a picture himself, and said it was a rattlesnake with a knot in its tail (fig. 8–6). When rattlesnakes were afraid they rattled enough to make you cover up

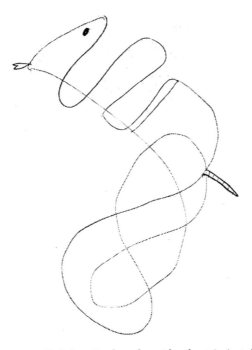

Fig. 8–6: Christian, Rattlesnake with a knot in its tail

your ears. Their fangs were not poisonous but it still hurt when they bit you. He had seen a film about this. "Do you know sidewinder snakes?" he asked then. They buried themselves in the sand and bit animals. They just had to be careful not to bite their own tails. There were nests with 15,000 birds in them and fire had broken out and all the birds had been burnt. Apes and elephants had eaten fermented fruit and got drunk. That was the mad world of animals, all sorts of mad things were told about them. I interpreted this to him as a story about his own situation. I said I thought that with him too something had had a knot in it; we had talked earlier about urine retention. He nodded.

In this way he had slowly drawn near to his theme: first the foot with the strange leaf, then the hand with an over-short middle finger and then the rollercoaster with the knotted H. And now this picture showed clearly and in a prominent position the knot in his tail, and the connection between fear and aggressiveness and between aggressiveness and the danger of turning it against yourself, catching yourself by the tail. I feel he formulated in these pictures what he had learnt about these connections in therapy.

The next picture was one he made out of my squiggle, and again it turned into a snake (fig. 8–7), a snake rearing up. It could see a picture up at the top with two (sic!) stick figures. Then he drew two more snakes, these were two carved snake brothers in the picture [top right], but they weren't supposed to be rolled up, but upright like the big snake. This was almost like Harry Potter, in the second volume [where there is a dangerous giant snake], or it looked like a ladder [at the bottom left]. I said that I saw we were now talking about snakes that were knotted up and afraid and snakes that stood upright. Christian then said snakes were his favourite animals. He also had a spider here, he said, the most poisonous spider, original size. The males were eaten by the females after they had fertilized them. I addressed the aggressive side in this situation and asked if he wasn't also a bit poisonous from time to time. He said that when his brother annoyed him he would put a blanket down on the floor, wait till he walked over it and then pull it out from under his feet. He'd fall over then, but not too hard.

Christian wanted to make his own picture out of his next scribble: again it was a snake, this time a 3-D snake (fig. 8–8). He told me he had learnt how to do that at school. I pointed out to him that I thought

Fig. 8–7: Christian, Snake rearing up

it was peeing, because there was something down there; there were drops coming out. He responded by asking if I knew how scorpions shit. They bent their tails up and did it on their backs. So we were still concerned with the diverse functions and dysfunctions of the penis and of excretion. In his next picture he drew another snake out of my squiggle (fig. 8–9). Here I addressed the sexual function directly and said I thought it looked like a tadpole or a sperm, they looked like that too. Yes, there was a film about that, he said, "Look who's talking". After that he carried on talking about spiders.

His next squiggle was also longish and I said I wasn't going to make a snake out of it but a string of lanterns (fig. 8–10). In his next

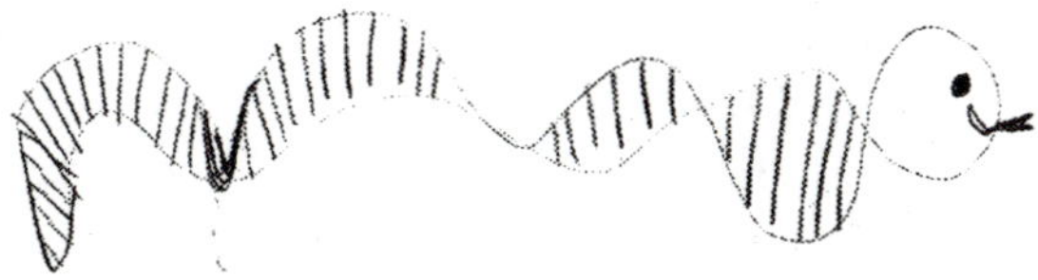

Fig. 8–8: Christian, 3-D snake

Fig. 8–9: Christian, Snake

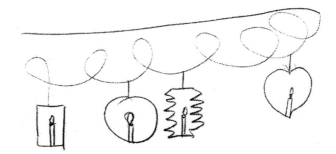

Fig. 8–10: Christian, String of lanterns

picture he picked up and elaborated the sexual theme which had been brought up with the sperm. He drew two worms (fig. 8–11) that loved each other. It was immediately obvious to me that one of the worms had a penis, admittedly drawn as an arm, but it looked quite serviceable. I commented that love was a nice thing to finish off with even if it was no longer like that with his parents. But he said he and his brother loved each other and both his father and his mother had new partners.

It seems to me that Christian was in a certain way summing up the insights he had drawn from his therapy, and once again depicting how he had had to deal intensively with the problem of his male identification, damage to it and how it functioned, including its self-destructive aspects. On the whole, our dialogue didn't seem to me

Fig. 8–11: Christian, Two worms that love each other

to be free of difficulties and conflicts, but the conversation gave me the impression that he now knew a lot more about himself, and could handle in a much more flexible and playful way the inner conflicts which had led him into such a dead end. When I first met him, he was on the verge of kidney failure due to his manifold psychic disturbances; now here was a boy who had begun to think about his ability to love. His ability to work was not so far advanced, according to his school report at the time of his discharge. He still seemed to be reserved and dreamy, so that despite normal intelligence his performance was impaired.

In his subsequent integration into home life, things worked quite well. The little wetting which remained was significantly reduced. Unfortunately the out-patient treatment we recommended did not take place. The mother said she found it quite uncomplicated with Christian at home. A little later Christian wrote us a postcard from his holidays saying he was fine and had no problems.

In this case the squiggle game enabled me to look again at the stage Christian's development had reached after this fairly long period of in-patient treatment. Christian made use of the interview to recapitulate his own development and his inner themes, and perhaps also to show me unconsciously how far he had got in working through his conflicts, but how much they were still a central theme in his inner world of experience. Because of their out-of-the-ordinary character, squiggle interviews are particularly suited to ascertaining how the therapy is going and what has been achieved. And especially because they are an unusual form of communication, they are registered by the child as having a special significance in the course of his therapy. In a case such as this one, there are also other factors: the imminent discharge, the unusualness of a conversation with the consultant, and the bond in the fact that we had met at the beginning.

But in any case, the squiggle game offers a good opportunity to use the pictures to share with and convey to the other members of the team what we were able to work on with the patient. This is something I hear from colleagues again and again: individual pictures from squiggle interviews, together with a discussion that fosters an understanding for the patient's inner situation, can act as a guiding light in treatment. It is easier to remember pictures which depict an inner problem in a way we can grasp than it is to remember some theoretical formulation which, despite being precise, often remains rather pale and needs to be brought alive. We shouldn't draw the wrong conclusion here: that the drawings are immediately understandable. It is only with a clear understanding of the development of a child and his inner conflicts that it becomes possible to work with the pictures and make the insights useful for the team. It goes without saying that showing tact towards the child, particularly if he has just depicted his problematic and vulnerable sides so openly, must be the maxim for any action taken.

For myself, I am again and again surprised at how closely the child's world of imagination can connect symptoms and unconscious conflicts in the squiggle drawings. All the knotted and biting snakes, over-short fingers and other defects point simultaneously to Christian's manifest main symptom and also to his castration anxiety and his aggressively-tinted identification with his father, with all its associated conflicts. Unconscious strivings of all kinds are densely interwoven, in the sense of an over-determination of the manifest contents. It is for this reason that the valid interpretation in each case emerges only in the dialogue between child and therapist: it stems from their work together.

CHAPTER NINE

How do sea monsters help against bed-wetting?

Jonathan, aged 11

W ith occasional interruptions, Jonathan was increasingly wetting his bed several times a week. After wetting his bed, he came over to his parents' bed and snuggled up to his father, wanting to be very close to him. According to the parents, even as a very small child he'd always been a "great one for snuggling", he came into their bed almost every night and snuggled up to his father. Jonathan was a bright boy, attending *Gymnasium* (academic secondary school) and performing well. Both parents were in academic professions. When Jonathan was two years old, there had been a change of childminder due to the family moving house; he seemed to have taken this in his stride.

Jonathan seemed fairly shy in the first two interviews, mentioning as problems only that if he got angry he liked to withdraw. He would read or not go out with family on trips at the weekend. He was sure that he would be able to cope with this bed-wetting and was motivated to do something about it. My impression was that he was putting himself under considerable pressure, and also wanted to do very well at school. He followed instructions like a good boy, particularly the one about not going to his parents' bed. The frequency of bed-wetting dropped considerably, but it didn't disappear altogether.

Since Jonathan did not accept the idea of therapy in the strict sense, we arranged to have occasional talks at intervals of two to three months. In our next conversation we found ourselves talking about puberty and his development, and he mentioned, rather short of breath and faltering, something about fears of what was going to happen to him. He said they laughed about it a lot in class but he didn't feel it was anything to laugh about. He nevertheless laughed along with the others. He was also in love with one of the girls in the class but he hadn't tried to have any closer contact with her. I talked to him in a bit more detail about his problems with development at puberty and he was clearly relieved; yet we didn't really make progress. The bed-wetting still kept occurring every two weeks or so. He urgently wanted this to change, but he didn't want to come to therapy regularly. In this stalemate the family had consulted a number of paediatricians, who had prescribed medication and pants with an alarm attached, with the result that Jonathan now resumed wetting his bed several times a week.

In one of our sessions I suggested a squiggle interview. Out of my first scribble he drew a phantasy animal (fig. 9–1). I was in the dark about what kind of phantasy this was and what drive elements were contained in it, but I did notice that the animal grew slimmer below the head and was wearing a kind of necklace. I didn't say anything about the animal at this stage. From his squiggle I made a big wave (fig. 9–2). I assume this idea of mine related equally to the storm that was brewing and to the symptom of bed-wetting. He took this up in his next picture, drawing an idyllic pond with water

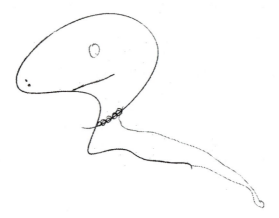

Fig. 9–1: Jonathan, Fantasy animal

Fig. 9–2: Jonathan, Great big wave

lilies (fig. 9–3). This made sense, and it is not unusual for children with enuresis to draw ponds like this. There was also something in this picture of an unexceptional, shy but certainly pleasant surface, whose depths could not easily be plumbed, that corresponded to Jonathan.

Fig. 9–3: Jonathan, Idyllic pond with water lilies

Our further dialogue centred on just this. From his squiggle I drew a pond in cross-section, with plants and fishes in it, and an observer up on a cliff, who was probably intended to represent me (fig. 9–4). Jonathan instantly took up this game and made a snail out of my squiggle (fig. 9–5), signalling that he could withdraw at any time, even if the snail had come out of its shell just now. Here too, it struck me how thin the tail end of the snail was. The snail also had no eyes, which I took to be an unconscious allusion to the fact that there was something that needed to be looked at but this seemed too difficult for him at the moment. In my next drawing I continued the theme of the snail and our game of coming out into the open and hiding by making a flash of lightning out of his suddenly fairly jagged squiggle (fig. 9–6), and added a snail, this time well-protected in its shell.

He took up the aggressive components, which had so far appeared in his behaviour only in the reversed forms of withdrawal and refusal, and drew a sea monster (fig. 9–7) armed with sharp teeth. His aggressive stirrings seemed to be coming closer to consciousness now in the course of our conversation, and after my implicit pictorial interpretation that withdrawal (snail in its shell) and aggression (lightning) might be related, he was able to allow some of this to

Fig. 9–4: Jonathan, Pond in section with plants and fishes

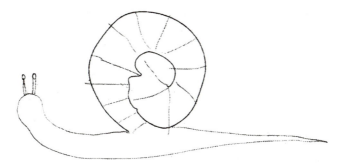

Fig. 9–5: Jonathan, Snail

Fig. 9–6: Jonathan, Flash of lightning and snail

come to the surface in his next squiggle drawing. The sea monster was rearing up out of the lake, out of the water (the urine?). It is possible that this cast a light on a much deeper layer of his problem: Jonathan had been weaned after six weeks when his mother went back to work; then at the age of two, as mentioned above, he had lost his childminder when they moved house. From here there was a connecting line to the striking way in which he always sought his father's side of the bed and snuggled up to him after wetting his bed, ignoring his mother. Presumably these events might be one

Fig. 9–7: Jonathan, Sea monster

source of his disappointment and his hidden anger about this disappointment. It might be that in the image of the sea monster he was also unconsciously depicting an oral-aggressive fixation based on these feelings. Jonathan may cautiously have approached these connections in this picture, even though at this point we were only talking very generally along the lines that this might have something to do with him. There was another striking thing about the sea monster. Once again the lower body was curiously malformed and looked somehow diffuse; it was also under the water line. We could conclude from this that the problem described above, the subjectively traumatic experience of disappointment in his mother and his subsequent avoidance of her, including ultimately repression of his oral-aggressive sides, had led to his making the father into a kind of substitute, which impaired and disturbed his identification with his father's male side. He snuggled with his father instead of becoming his rival, as would be appropriate at his age (he was now twelve).

Continuing the story of his sea monster, I drew a tightrope walker balancing over a lake in which there was a fish with very sharp teeth (fig. 9–8). Thus I took up both components of the sea monster motif, the visible and the invisible, and told him in my drawing that I understood this to be a difficult balancing act for him, which might impede or endanger his development as he moved up along the rope. His next picture, and the last of the session, was a nice boy (fig. 9–9).

Fig. 9–8: Jonathan, Tightrope walker

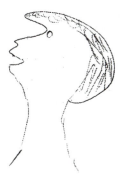

Fig. 9–9: Jonathan, Nice boy

We could ask ourselves if he was returning in this picture to his defence organization of the nice, shy boy, which had so far been stable and largely functioned successfully. There is certainly an element of this in the picture. Often children show a remarkable ability to cover up the partly-revealed unconscious layers again in their last picture, in order to be able to end the session. On the other hand, this boy he had drawn looked too open to me—he was speaking and looking ahead—to be seen as a mere return to the old pattern. And indeed a conversation then developed between us about these drawings. We were able to talk about the fact that different parts of his self were represented in the different figures, and he said that on the surface he was mostly a nice boy, smiling and friendly, but sometimes he wanted to be as big and strong as the sea monster. He was also often as slow as the snail and wanted to be quicker, which I related to the problem of his development. To round it off I also reminded him of his withdrawal behaviour, which was like that of the snail, but pointed out that he might sometimes also want to be as vicious as the sea-monster. In doing this I avoided any interpretation of the conflict that might have gone too deep, orienting myself mainly to the manifest material relatively close to consciousness. An unconscious communication was established between us during the squiggle game. At the same time, I am fairly sure that I would not have been able to formulate an interpretation of these deeper levels during the session. Apart from this, an interpretation would not have served any purpose. It would have impeded rather than facilitated the deeper contact which had only just been established between us.

After this session I again offered Jonathan regular therapy. He argued against it, citing lack of time, and said he would rather take up a martial art, for instance karate, and continue to come to me from time to time. After that we had about another five sessions over longer intervals in which we mainly played Tipp-Kick [a table-top football game] or darts. He threw himself into these games, coming out of himself and competing with me. The parents reported that previously Jonathan had always been anxious to maintain harmony. If his mother had, for instance, had an argument with his brother, who was two years older, it had always been dreadful for Jonathan. In the meantime, they said, he had begun to argue with his father more. Once his father had shouted at him, saying he was behaving like a four-year old, and Jonathan had objected equally fiercely that *he* was behaving like an 84-year-old. The bed-wetting ceased permanently after a short time, and we agreed to end our sessions. In the subsequent years, Jonathan's development proceeded without any major psychological problems.

We can see from this case vignette how quickly unconscious layers can appear in a squiggle interview. In terms of technique for therapeutic procedure this does not necessarily mean that they should be interpreted in every situation. It often turns out to be better in such short therapeutic encounters to work along the line of the defence formations, the more so since, as in the case of Jonathan, we can also count on the self-healing and developmental forces in the child, once certain barriers have been cleared away by means of our intervention. The beginner can easily run the risk of becoming so enthusiastic about the insights the game offers that he or she interprets too much, which can destroy the free flow of communication. There are some interpretations we make for our own use, whether to assure ourselves of the correctness of our theories, or out of enthusiasm over what we have recognised, or because we are disconcerted by the elements in the child's communication that we have not understood. This was what Winnicott meant when he wrote in *Therapeutic Consultations in Child Psychiatry* that one will discover that the interpretation of the unconscious is not in the foreground. Nothing is harder than to explain why we have made no interpretation over an extended period of time, or even throughout the interview, and then at a particular moment used the material to interpret the unconscious. "It would seem almost as if one has to tolerate the existence of two contrary trends in oneself." (Winnicott, 1971a, p. 9)

With this material and the different strands of interpretation that have been touched on here, we can easily see what multi-layered possibilities there are to construct meaningful connections from the material. This has to do with the over-determination of all psychical process. Over and above this, pictorial material is particularly subject to processes of condensation and displacement, as Freud first described comprehensively in *The Interpretation of Dreams*. It is often hard to describe which strands, and for what reason, are picked out by the therapist to test. The choice will have something to do with the therapist's personality, unconscious conflicts and experience, that is to say what we call countertransference in the strict sense. If a dialogue can be established, then this choice is significantly determined by a mutual "tuning in", which has often been described as communication from unconscious to unconscious. The analyst picks up the fine verbal messages from the child, and even more the non-verbal ones, modifies his tuning to the child and the focus of his interpretations according to these perceptions.

CHAPTER TEN

The king's castle, the mother's rucksack. The wish for the Other on facing death

Klaus, aged 8/10

Klaus was an eight-year-old boy when I first met him. He was suffering from a neuroblastoma, a malignant tumour of the nerve tissues. He was to be admitted to the children's clinic for a bone marrow transplant. The family was socially isolated, the mother came from a different culture and did not speak German particularly well. The boy had had practically no social contact with his peer group as a result of his illness, as I discovered after the first interview. He had been to kindergarten only for a few months before becoming ill; he had not gone on to attend school. When we met for the first time about a week before his planned admission, he seemed withdrawn, lacking in vitality and anxiously reserved. The first squiggle pictures were characterised by the fact that parts of the lower body were missing: in some cases the animals had no legs. Interspersed were pictures in which body parts were twisted, and there were indications of a psychic dedifferentiation. Gradually I managed to get into conversation with the boy. He began to open up a little and talked about how sad he was to be so isolated socially, while his younger sister was able to go to school. He opened up to the point of being able to speak about his fear of what was to come. Towards the end of our conversation he seemed increasingly to have rebuilt his encircling wall, and drew as his final picture (fig. 10–1) a person with a lot of hair—just think of chemotherapy and the associated loss of hair—whose legs seemed, however, to be missing.

Fig. 10–1: Klaus, Person with a lot of hair

On my asking about this, he said they were wrapped in a blanket. We agreed that this was a person completely wrapped up in a blanket and therefore a baby. This interpretation made him laugh with relief. He was obviously able for a moment to identify completely with regressive wishes. When I asked my colleagues afterwards, I was told that the illness had indeed at times caused him pain in the legs. But above all, the boy was unconsciously using this image as a metaphor for his bleak situation, robbed as it was psychologically of all possible movement.

In the second interview four weeks later, a week and half after the transplant, we were talking in Klaus' isolation room on the transplant ward. For his last picture he drew a child sleeping (fig. 10–2). This child also had no legs, and in addition the body image was largely undifferentiated. Clinically he displayed a depressive withdrawal, lying in bed all day and sleeping.

I saw Klaus for a third interview just three years after the transplant. He was now 10 years old and knew at this point that he would soon die. None of his treatment had brought about the desired result, there had been two relapses, and there remained nothing else that could be done with the tumour. However, he had never spoken a word either to his mother or to the doctors treating him about his situation and imminent death, but had withdrawn into himself.

Fig. 10–2: Klaus, Sleeping child

Looking at my first squiggle, nothing occurred to him. This corresponded completely with the anxious and cautious attitude he was showing. Out of his first squiggle I drew a girl, thinking briefly that she was actually dancing. Looking back, I think I was already inwardly preoccupied with his situation, caught between keeping his distance and needing contact. Against this background, the girl could be seen as a kind of compromise between offering a relationship and not making too direct a reference to him or his situation. Presumably this picture also had to do with an almost manic defence on my part, such as we often use in moments when we are trying to cope with the threat of death and the associated fears in patients with a fatal illness: rather a dancing girl than a fatally ill boy. Fairly quickly Klaus then drew "something you can push", as he said, out of my squiggle (fig. 10–3). In the end he settled for it being a mouse. Push-along toys like this are generally for three-year-olds rather than ten-year-olds, so I assumed that this was a depiction of pronounced regressive wishes. When I entered into this childish level with a picture of a bear (fig. 10–4), he began to bring another side to the fore. First of all he drew a bird (fig. 10–5), and we talked about how it could fly far away and soar up high, and was strong. Finally it occurred to him that the wings were missing, and he added them. I understood this picture of a bird soaring up as expression of his preoccupation with his approaching death, and as the beginning of an indirect conversation with me on this subject. The missing wings and the narcissistically tinged phantasy of being strong and soaring up in flight showed the inner stirring of feelings as he approached the subject. We could add here that the picture shows neuropsychological deficits connected to his illness in the visual

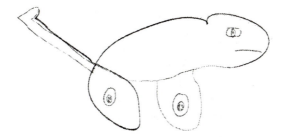

Fig. 10–3: Klaus, Mouse that you can push along

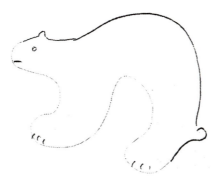

Fig. 10–4: Klaus, Bear

Fig. 10–5: Klaus, Bird

processing, for instance in the incorrect positioning of the body parts, but I will not go into detail here on this aspect of the drawing.

I reacted with reserve in sketching a vase with flowers (fig. 10–6), their heads hanging a little perhaps. I wanted to wait and see how the process would develop on Klaus' side; he was taking the lead in terms of the pace and depth of our contact, and I certainly didn't want to endanger this with an over-hasty interpretation. What followed was another picture showing his phantasy of strength: a football boot (fig. 10–7). We talked about football, and he told me

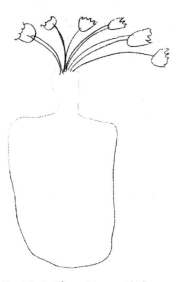

Fig. 10–6: Klaus, Vase with flowers

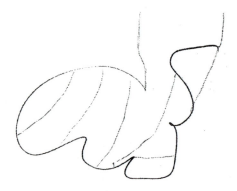

Fig. 10–7: Klaus, Football boot

that he liked to going to school and had played football and scored a lot of goals. All of these were in fact things that had not been possible on account of his illness and isolation. My picture from his next scribble depicted a mighty, ancient tree (fig. 10–8). I was presumably still preoccupied with the theme of life span and death. His next picture was a rain cloud with a flash of lightning (fig. 10–9). I thought of the threat his illness represented, but wasn't sure if he wanted to go on to make this our subject, and so drew a harmless butterfly out of his squiggle (fig. 10–10).

From my next scribble Klaus finally drew a king (fig. 10–11), which I took to be a narcissistic phantasy with the power to protect him. Taking this up in my next picture, I turned his squiggle, again

Fig. 10–8: Klaus, Old, mighty tree

Fig. 10–9: Klaus, Rain cloud with flash of lightning

Fig. 10–10: Klaus, Butterfly

without much thought, into the (protective) wall of the king's castle (fig. 10–12), with a great gate. He laughed at this and was pleased. This entering into what he had drawn in our communication by pictures seemed to encourage him to seek closer contact with me, because he now began, working very meticulously, to draw an animal out of my scribble (fig. 10–13), an animal climbing up

Fig. 10–11: Klaus, King

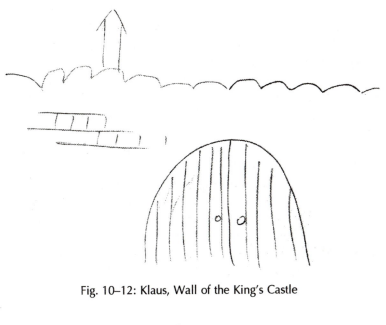

Fig. 10–12: Klaus, Wall of the King's Castle

Fig. 10–13: Klaus, Animal climbing up somewhere with small
animal in its rucksack

somewhere. It might have been climbing up this wall. In its rucksack this animal had a small animal, which was afraid of falling down. I saw in this a depiction of his no-escape situation and so addressed it, saying that you could see the little animal was afraid. Perhaps, I continued, the only thing that would help the little animal would be for the big one to hold it really tight. He agreed with this interpretation. He was perceptibly involved now and maintaining intense contact with me.

At this point I suggested that each of us should draw one more picture. From his scribble I drew a boy (fig. 10–14), thus returning to the beginning, and gave him my interpretation that I understood this was all about him. Klaus then drew his last picture, once again working meticulously (fig. 10–15). The person on the peak had climbed up the ladder on the right, and there was now a fire blocking his way back. Originally there had been a rope to hold on to at the side of the path. He added this a little later. I talked to him about how the person up there could be helped. He answered: "If another person was there." I encouraged him to draw this other person and he drew a slightly bigger figure with a suitcase at the bottom. This person was coming to help. There were ropes and things in there. I was deeply impressed by this very realistic depiction of his situation: he had climbed too high, couldn't get out, and realised that he was lost. I don't think we should interpret the possibility of rescue depicted in the picture at this point as a phantasy that a rescue was actually feasible. Instead it seemed to me that the picture showed

Fig. 10–14: Klaus, Boy

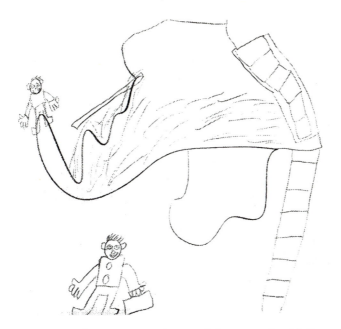

Fig. 10–15: Klaus, Person at the top of the mountain with fire

forcefully that he needed someone to be with him. Thus in his picture at this point in our conversation, Klaus formulated his realistic assessment of the situation, his fear of death and his wish for closeness. It would have been tactless, even harmful to talk about it in detail at this point in the conversation. We had both understood what was meant.

Klaus' mother had been so unsettled and afraid that she had not dared to speak to her son openly about his situation. Their relationship, which had always been quite close and seemed to offer protection against an environment perceived as threatening, had intensified over the course of his illness, so that often there was little space for anything or anyone else. But now their inability to talk about the mortal danger threatening the boy had intensified and worsened the dynamics of their relationship. Klaus clung to his mother on the one hand, but for her part, she felt that he was not really allowing her to get close to him any more. He was even less able to make contact with other people, and instead largely withdrew. Like a good boy he followed the instructions given him by the doctors and nurses in the clinic, but people increasingly found him depressed and lifeless. After our conversation I talked to his mother and described how it had gone. With the help of the pictures I was able to demonstrate to her how important her presence was to the boy and how important it was to talk to him openly about his situation, his fears and his grief. She found the courage to do this and spoke to him more openly in the subsequent days. This meant that the two of them spent a very intensive time together in the last weeks of his life, which was a great relief for the mother and allowed Klaus to take his leave.

Therapeutic work with patients facing death is threatened by nameless dread and also by speechlessness. Children are barely able to speak about their fears and despair because they feel they have to protect their parents, and they register their parents' fear and avoidance of the theme very clearly. The doctors and nurses treating such patients are often not able to accept this side of a child. They often have to look after many children who are about to die, and in order to maintain their own psychological balance it is necessary for them not to expose themselves fully time and again to the immeasurable fears threatening a child. Moreover, they are identified with their task of healing as long as there is hope rather than with an intense concern with death, which could easily look like giving up too soon and might therefore harm the patient in their care. The result is that this task is often left to third parties, whether the staff of the psychosocial services or the clinic chaplain or, in cases where the children show reactions of severe stress, child therapists and child psychiatrists.

The squiggle game is an opportunity to enter into contact with such children in that it offers a different kind of dialogue where speechlessness has set in, and makes it far easier for the children to allow themselves to enter into a relationship. The therapist, too, is somewhat protected at the outset, in that he knows they will both have something to do, and that if he follows the rhythm of the child, an approach to the theme of death may gradually emerge. Particularly in such encounters, the relieving function of activity should not be underestimated. Being able to do something—even just drawing—counters the unbearable feelings of helplessness and exposure in both child and therapist, and makes it easier for them to get into conversation.

In addition, the pictures make it easier to convey to the parents, and in some cases also to the doctors and nursing staff, what we were able to work out in the interview with the child. In my experience, something they can see for themselves seems to be easier to understand and makes a deeper impression. The interpretation gains credibility when it is supported by pictures, and this is extremely important with regard to the previously mentioned fears of the parents and the medical team. Last but not least, it is the individual pictures characterizing the inner situation of the child that become fixed in the memory of the parents and the medical team, thereby enabling a permanent change in their interaction at this decisive time, as was possible with Klaus.

CHAPTER ELEVEN

Ghosts, babies and Chinese porcelain cups. Fear, fragility and the wish to be beautiful

Elke, aged 10/13

I examined 10-year-old Elke within the framework of a research project on coping mechanisms shown by children aged between 8 and 12 during bone marrow transplantation (Günter, Werning, Karle & Klingebiel, 1997; Günter, 2000; Günter, 2002; Günter, 2003). In Chapter 14 I describe some of the results of this work in more detail. In order to give a better understanding of the situation in which Elke found herself, I will briefly describe the process of a bone marrow transplant. Again, a more detailed account can be found in Chapter 14. Elke had developed severe aplastic anaemia a few months before, which meant that she required regular blood transfusions; without a successful bone marrow or stem cell transplant, the condition is fatal. She was now undergoing further extensive diagnostic examinations in the clinic after the indication for the bone marrow transplant had been confirmed. My first squiggle interview with Elke took place in my office at the clinic in the week before her admission for the planned bone marrow transplant. A week later Elke was admitted, and the first procedure she underwent was conditioning, that is to say the removal of the remaining bone marrow through the administration of large doses of cytostatic drugs. About a week after her admission, the transplant was carried out in the form of an intravenous infusion of bone marrow via a Hickman catheter. During this time and for the following three weeks, Elke, like other children in the same situation, had to be treated in a germ-free environment, in a single room under isolation conditions. With the removal of the bone marrow, the body's immune defences were largely eliminated and there was a risk of lethal infection until the new bone marrow had grafted in. Our second interview took place in this isolation room on the 18th day after the transplant. The third interview was roughly three years after her first transplant. I visited Elke at her home after agreeing on an appointment with her. It was not until the end of this interview that I learnt from her that in the meantime she had suffered a relapse and had to receive a second transplant. She said she had forgotten when this second transplant had taken place. If she should suffer a second relapse, she told me she would not agree to undergo another transplant.

Elke was the eldest of three children (she had two younger brothers) in an ethnic German family which had resettled from Russia three years before. She was a reserved and shy child, very anxious to co-operate well with the doctors and nurses, and also with me. She was very proud of her thick, long, dark blonde hair, which she wore in a plait and which was destined to fall out in the course of the transplant. The main person Elke related to was her mother, who for her part had great difficulty battling her own fears and grief over the development of Elke's illness, and needed much encouragement and support. The father was largely out of the picture. The squiggle interviews can only be given here in abridged form, since we drew 25 pictures in the first, 23 in the second and 19 in the final encounter.

Squiggle 1, a week before admission for bone marrow transplantation

In her first pictures Elke several times brought up the theme of something being missing, of there being some defect. It was clear that she was unconsciously trying to compensate for this defect. Among other things she linked this with the subject of hair: many of the figures had no hair. Alongside these pictures there were also ones in which the figures didn't function well. In the further course of the interview she depicted this conflict in narcissistically-tinged phantasies of a complete restoration of her femininity. Throughout the interview, ball dresses and pink ribbons etc. kept making an appearance. This theme was interrupted by a bear which wanted to

Fig. 11–1: Elke, Bear that frightens people

run away and which frightened people (fig. 11–1, picture 11 in the interview). That was a picture which was very important to her. From my point of view it was multiply determined. As I interpreted it, she was localizing her fear projectively in other people. At the same time, in this bear running away she was expressing her own wish to get away from the situation. And finally, what was already appearing to emerge here—in contrast to her seemingly very well-adapted behaviour—was a further element of her identity containing some aggressive and cheeky momentum. I also had the impression, for which I couldn't seem to find clear reasons, that Elke was hinting in this picture at an unconscious phantasy that she only had problems of this kind and an illness of this nature because she was a girl. Presumably, though, the picture also had something to do with her home country and the identity which was rooted there.

She referred to the fox in my next picture as a wolf, thereby intensifying the already present theme of danger. After all, as we know from folk tales, wolves are animals which devour people. She continued the theme of danger a few pictures later in the form of a ghost with a markedly defective, damaged body shape (fig. 11–2, picture 15 in the interview), and then went on to draw a ghost showing its muscles (fig. 11–3, picture 17 in the interview), an unconscious narcissistic defence phantasy that offered her protection. She formulated the threat which she related to her sex most clearly

Fig. 11–2: Elke, Ghost

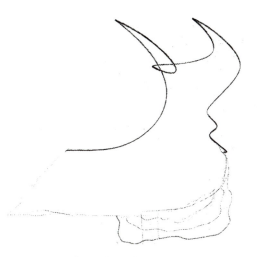

Fig. 11–3: Elke, Ghost showing its muscles

later on, after we had talked about her brothers, one of whom was the bone marrow donor. She drew a picture of a bird on its nest with two eggs (fig. 11–4, picture 21 in the interview) and commented that both the young were going to be boys, male birds. She as a girl felt threatened by death, while the boys were safe in the nest. Her next picture further underlined this interpretation and cautiously suggested hope for herself. She concluded our interview with a picture that signalled harmlessness, and so reconstituted the defence

Fig. 11–4: Elke, Bird in a nest with two eggs

Fig. 11–5: Elke, Cat playing with wool

she needed in this situation: it showed a cat playing with a ball of wool (fig. 11–5, picture 25 in the interview).

Squiggle 2, four weeks later, day 18 after the bone marrow transplant

Elke instantly took up her theme of clothes from our first conversation (ribbons, ball gowns, etc). But now, right in the foreground of her very first picture, she was dealing with what was missing inside the body of the figure. This theme was continued in the following pictures: the figures appeared inwardly empty and defective. By way of a further intermediate step, she arrived logically at a depiction of what was unconsciously preoccupying her, what she lacked in her unconscious phantasy: a baby. She drew a snake which was so fat because it was carrying a baby (fig. 11–6, picture 7 in the interview), followed by a boy (fig. 11–7, picture 9 in the interview), and then a ghost (fig. 11–8, picture 11 in the interview) which—it emerged from our conversation—was sad because it didn't have anyone to scare. The phantasy which had only been hinted at in the first interview three weeks earlier was now shown more clearly: a phantasy which she had initially had to repress, that there was a fundamental defect in her body. According to this phantasy, there would be no problems if she were a cheeky boy and not a girl.

Fig. 11–6: Elke, Pregnant snake

Fig. 11–7: Elke, Boy

This theme was repeated once more. Elke drew another boy, who this time was sticking out his tongue (fig. 11–9, picture 17 in the interview); his hair was noticeably very emphatic. A second possible way of overcoming fear and depression could be seen in scaring others (as with the squiggle of the ghost, and very similarly with the bear in the first interview): in other words the fear was projectively

Fig. 11–8: Elke, Sad ghost

Fig. 11–9: Elke, Boy sticking out his tongue

localized in others and thus warded off. She tied this theme in with the depictions of girls with long hair which have already been mentioned. On this point it must be remembered that there was a very real connection here: she loved her long, thick hair and was deeply distressed over its loss in the course of the conditioning. She focused the interview more and more firmly on the struggle with this defect and on the connection between the aggressive nature of the illness and the fear she felt (snake and shivering mouse, fig. 11–10, picture 15 in the interview). Elke continued with the theme of defects in her body, and in the end she was able to approach her deeply depressive side and to express it in only slightly veiled form. The ghost in the final picture (fig. 11–11, picture 23 in the interview)

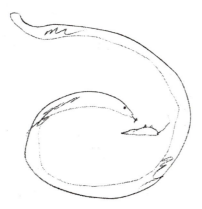

Fig. 11–10: Elke, Snake and shivering mouse

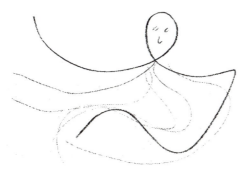

Fig. 11–11: Elke, Ghost

would like to be a real person and was very sad that it lacked so much, she said herself. This emotional opening, though, was accompanied by a loss of contour and form in the body image. What had been kept in shape with great effort was now threatening to lose its shape.

In the second interview Elke was able to present more openly the central theme of her situation and her phantasy life, its threatening nature and the extent of its emptiness. Her defence formations against this emptiness and threat also seemed to be more precisely related to the theme and therefore more functional despite all the stress placed on them. Thus in her final picture at the end of the interview, she was able to find not only pictorial but also verbal expression for her inner world and what was threatening her. As a result, in our second interview she seemed better able to cope with the fears and conflicts triggered by the life-threatening illness and the treatment with its side-effects, and she was able to integrate them into her personality and defence structures despite the acute stress of treatment in isolation.

Squiggle 3, three years later

Elke began with the face of a ghost (fig. 11–12, picture 1 in the interview), thus picking up the thread of our earlier squiggles. It occurred to me that she was perhaps haunted by the spectre of a relapse. I reacted with a girl in a cap because I remembered how important her hair had been to her. Out of the next squiggle she drew

Fig. 11–12: Elke, Face of a ghost

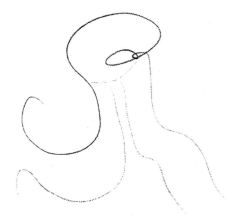

Fig. 11–13: Elke, Jellyfish

a jellyfish (fig. 11–13, picture 3 in the interview), and told me that jellyfish could hold on with their tentacles. She had heard that they were dying out. I was a little confused for moment and asked her if she meant polyps, but she insisted that this was a jellyfish. I took this as a continuation of the previous picture and as a depiction of her vulnerability in a situation which remained threatening for her. She did indeed say later in the conversation that if it were possible she would like to forget all about it, but she knew she couldn't since she would have to go back for check-ups for the rest of her life. In this context she herself used the word "fragile" several times.

Her next picture showed an extra-terrestrial with a peculiar hairstyle (fig. 11–14, picture 5 in the interview). The further course of the interview showed that she had been preoccupied with the question of whether, by virtue of the transplantation of bone marrow from her brother, she might have become someone else, perhaps a male or even an extra-terrestrial. I reacted, without being conscious of this thought at the time, by drawing the head of a boy. She responded with a picture of a girl with long, wavy hair, whose pointed nose she accentuated. Then out of my next squiggle she drew a finger puppet (fig. 11–15, picture 9 in the interview) and we talked about her having had finger puppets like that during her time in the clinic. But they had fallen apart in the meantime and she had thrown them away, she said. In my next picture I also referred to her time in the clinic by drawing a glove out of her squiggle. Elke's next phantasy animal (fig. 11–16, picture 11 in the interview) had, she explained to me, the neck of a snake, the fur of a dog, and as to the other parts, she didn't know where they came from. So here she was continuing the theme of change of identity in a different form. My next picture, a snake, took up her explanation. Next she drew a bird whose head was far too round, and only at this point did it dawn

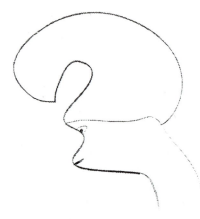

Fig. 11–14: Elke, Extra-terrestrial being

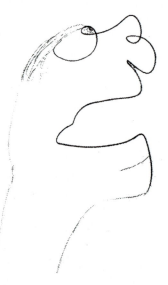

Fig. 11–15: Elke, Finger puppet

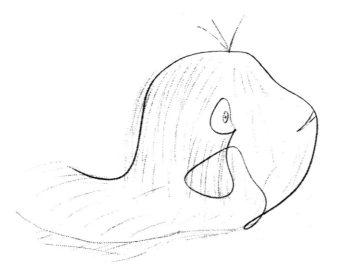

Fig. 11–16: Elke, Fantasy animal with the neck of a snake
and the fur of a dog

on me that all her drawings were concerned with heads: ghost's head,
jellyfish (practically all head), extra-terrestrial head, girl's head,
finger puppet, head of a phantasy animal (with neck). I assumed that
in depicting the outward appearance of the head and how it changed
she was also referring to the inner change which had taken place in
her head as a result of her illness and its radical treatment. It is
important to realise that children's hair falls out in the course of high
dose chemotherapy, and that for most of them this is not only the
most visible outward sign of their illness but also often a fact on
which they pin their inner struggle with their illness and the fears
and narcissistic wounds associated with it. In Elke's case, this was
compounded by the fact that she had been particularly proud of her
hair, and also by the fact that in the first months of her illness (which
is when her change began) she had been treated with high doses of
cortisone and as a result had developed Cushing's syndrome and
with it an extremely rounded face.

So in the next four pictures we concerned ourselves with various
heads: I drew a really beautiful rhino head with a large horn, she
drew the head of a boy looking angry or scared. My next was a cute
little dog's head, and after that Elke drew the head and upper body

of a ghost wearing spectacles (fig. 11–17, picture 17 in the interview), which I felt had a very threatening quality in that no eyes were visible. I suggested that he must have lived in the past, thereby of course implicitly referring to the history of her illness, which seemed to give her such a fright that she very quickly said that there were no such things as ghosts really. Her next squiggle seemed very structured to me, and I went along with this and made a very simple vase, which in this case presumably suggested a container for her tangible fright a moment earlier. She took up this idea and made her last picture one of a Chinese porcelain cup (fig. 11–18, picture 19 in the interview). We then spoke about the lovely ornament, which she coloured in beautifully, and about how fragile she was.

Elke and her parents told me after this third interview (which was three years after her first transplant) that she had reintegrated well socially after the transplants. At school all was going well, she had been top of the class last year. She wanted to become a nursery school teacher but would like after leaving her present school to go to the *Realschule* and get the higher qualifications there. The extremely good

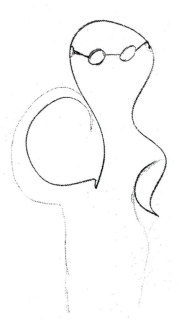

Fig. 11–17: Elke, Ghost with glasses

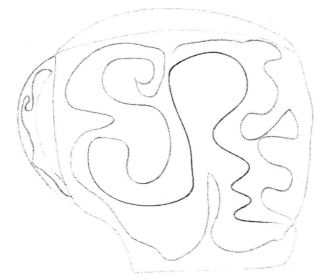

Fig. 11–18: Elke, Chinese porcelain cup

outward social adaptation—which we often see after such severe illnesses—could not, on closer examination, disguise the fact that Elke, like many other children, was still intensely preoccupied with the extreme threat to her narcissistic stability and integrity and with the permanent fear of a relapse. One theme which is of great significance at a much earlier stage for girls than for boys also represented a serious problem for Elke. She told me after our squiggle interview at the end of the examination that she didn't know whether she would be able to have children or whether the treatment had made her sterile. She wanted to have four children, two girls and two boys. But she wasn't going to ask about that yet, she would do it when she was older.

The conversations show how great a discrepancy there can be between an almost perfect adaptation first to the need for some extremely difficult and protracted therapy and then to social realities on the one hand, and the inner world of experience on the other hand. In their everyday life, it is usually not possible for these children to talk about their fears, their feelings of being inferior and defective, and their narcissistic injuries, which are often as hard to bear as the physical impairments and the dangers. Nor would talking about these things serve any purpose, we may assume, since it would involve the risk of destabilizing their hard-won psychological balance and might lead to fresh emotional injuries. Defence processes have the power to protect these very sick children and to facilitate their psychosocial adaptation. I would thus like to state emphatically that contrary to a widespread misunderstanding of psychoanalytical theory, defence processes should not be regarded primarily as pathological phenomena but seen as necessary and as a rule helpful coping strategies. Only if there is a rigidity, a restriction in the flexibility of these defence processes, in particular where "primitive" defence mechanisms are predominant, can we conclude that there is a pathological condition, either because the patient is severely overtaxed in his or her current situation or because of a pre-existing neurotic disorder.

The problem that faces us as psychotherapists, psychoanalysts or psychiatrists of children when we see patterns of coping that have gone off the rails is that the children will often still cling tightly to their story that they are fine, they have no wish at all to speak to anyone about their problems, and anyway they don't have any. I have found the squiggle game extremely helpful especially in such difficult situations with children who have very severe or life-threatening illnesses. To most children the game appears so unobtrusive that they can often put aside their anxiety that their well-hidden worst fears, anger and despair might be dragged out into the light. The diffuse fear of not being able to handle these things once they are dragged out, and of being left alone with them, often gives way very quickly to a trusting opening up which we would scarcely have expected. I am constantly amazed by the sophisticated way Elke was able to depict her inner life using the pictures of animals and other things, and by how sophisticated and multifaceted psychic life can be even under conditions of extreme threat to life. Particularly in the hardest of clinical situations, the squiggle game offers an immensely valuable way of entering into a conversation with a child, one in which her innermost fears, conflicts and injuries are touched on but at the same time her defence options remain intact.

With Elke it was not a case of therapeutic intervention in the real sense, but I often find that the squiggle game helps to restrict primitive and dysfunctional defence mechanisms and replace them with more mature forms of defence. If the child can become more flexible in handling her defences—and this is often the outcome of such contact with sick children who have landed in deep psychological crisis—then for the moment much, and in some cases everything, is gained. The long-term psychotherapy which may be needed can then begin once the situation is no longer life-threatening and the child and her family are back to "normal".

CHAPTER TWELVE

Scribbling as an activity done together: squiggle pictures as tangible objects in the outside world

Heinz, aged 15

Heinz was a 15-year-old boy who had withdrawn almost totally from any contact outside the family. He did go to school, but was socially an outsider who was only tolerated to prevent his being even further isolated. Instead of speaking he would make barking sounds interspersed with a few words. Only when he was furious was he able briefly to speak in full sentences. His intellectual abilities were not impaired, as had been shown by a test a few years earlier. A period of in-patient adolescent psychiatric treatment had been cut short by the family because Heinz had become homesick, and his mother could also no longer bear to be separated from him. Heinz suffered from a marked infantile autism.

As to his earlier history, it was reported that Heinz had been difficult even as a newborn and throughout his infancy, with frequent bouts of screaming. Even then he had been conspicuously slow. He didn't walk until he was two or talk until he was four, and had difficulties with articulation right from the start. Already at kindergarten his withdrawal from social contact had caused difficulties.

At home the situation had come to a head in the preceding months. The parents reported that he had recently become aggressive more frequently, shouting and slamming doors. Later in the conversation it turned out that he had once cycled through the village wearing a black face mask and firing a replica pistol. He had been taken to the police. He had also taken to starting fires; as it turned out, he was trying to smoke out voles. The parents had decided to bring Heinz to me as an out-patient initially, with a view to determining whether in-patient treatment would be sensible or possible.

In our conversation Heinz came across as very tense, and at times he gave the impression of being dominated by inner fears. With me too, in answer to questions he only managed to blurt out yes or no, interspersed with other sounds. He couldn't make eye contact. Often his eyes were sweeping round the room, and his hands were constantly restless. If he did utter a word in addition to yes or no, it was unclear and slurred.

Given that only such minimal verbal contact was possible, I decided to offer Heinz a variant of the squiggle game in order to make contact in this way. It was clear from the start that he would not be able to allow himself to enter fully into an exchange of the kind that normally emerges in a squiggle game, and indeed these sessions, in which we did drawings, deviated in several respects from the "normal" course of a squiggle game. Firstly, we didn't each make a drawing out of the other's squiggle. On the contrary, it was very soon clear that Heinz, with his autistic-obsessive personality structure, attached great importance to our working together on one piece of paper the whole time. Another difference was that talking about the drawings, as normally happens in a squiggle game, was possible with Heinz only in very rudimentary terms. The purpose of the game is above all to set up a dialogue in pictures which eventually leads to communication in speech. Thus in our exchange some of the central elements that make up the squiggle game were missing. I nevertheless thought it worthwhile to include this case vignette because here too, the events were in essence determined by a wish to make some form of emotional contact with the child. I leave it to the reader to decide how far this succeeded.

When I suggested the squiggle game to Heinz, the atmosphere between us relaxed perceptibly. Whether it was that I had a better feeling about being with him, or whether he was relieved that this way he would not be confronted too directly with my demands and expectations but could concentrate on this business of drawing something together, at any rate we both seemed happier with this way of communicating. I had the distinct impression that this relaxation resulted quite quickly in his establishing a contact with me and that a dialogue emerged.

In the first session (fig. 12–1) we drew more or less alongside each other's lines using a sheet of A3 paper for our squiggle game. In the next session a fortnight later, Heinz already began to connect up some of his lines to mine (fig. 12–2), and I fell in with this. This pattern was intensified in the third session (fig. 12–3), so that we now often took it in turns to extend a line. In the fourth and last of Heinz's out-patient sessions, he finally began to imitate my structures, for example a spiral line and other graphic figures (fig. 12–4), so that I felt that we were genuinely beginning to relate to one another.

This method of communicating stabilized increasingly after Heinz was admitted as an in-patient. In the sessions that followed, he retained the pattern of joining his lines to mine. In response I extended his lines, so that bit by bit our "dialogue" became distinctly more playful. An example of this is fig. 12–5, which was drawn in our second session following Heinz's admission. For the first time, closed and separate figures emerged, which we had created together. In the following sessions, Heinz oriented his drawing partly to mine and often imitated my movements. In this form of interplay some

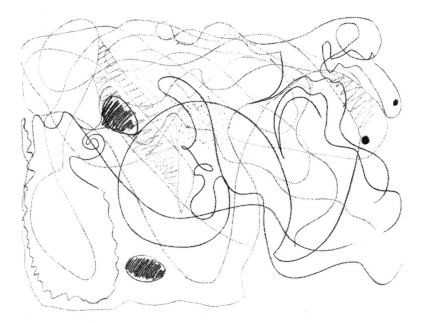

Fig. 12–1: Heinz

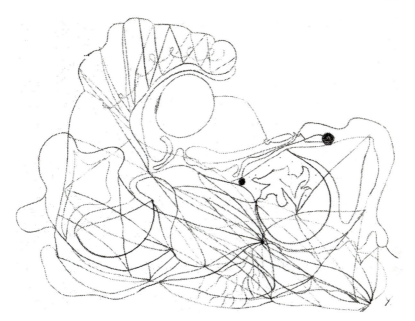

Fig. 12–2: Heinz

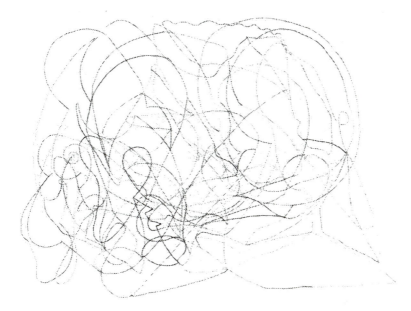

Fig. 12–3: Heinz

Fig. 12–4: Heinz

Fig. 12–5: Heinz

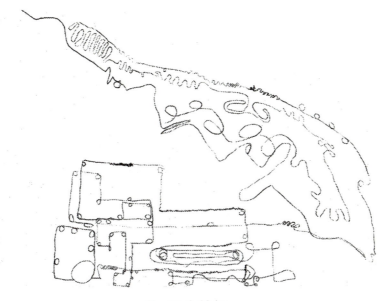

Fig. 12–6: Heinz

ornamental forms developed, as in our sixth session following his admission (fig. 12–6). By the end of the session we had produced something almost like an electronic circuit diagram, though in some respects this appeared very obsessive. Likewise Heinz's strong tendency to imitate in the next session—but now he was drawing somewhat chaotic and stronger lines too (fig. 12–7). In subsequent pictures this one-dimensional work was superseded by a more two-dimensional depiction and conception. Whereas in the previous pictures the main principle of communication had been represented initially by the lines in themselves, and then by Heinz joining his lines to mine and imitating mine, now he too was producing some rudimentary ornamentation. The result was that the paper was no longer being more or less evenly covered with lines (fig. 12–8, 9th session) but areas of ornamentation now appeared, which in part also reflected territorial demarcation and border disputes between us (fig. 12–9, 13th session).

In the following period we moved on to other things, and for Heinz an extended period of in-patient treatment followed. Interestingly enough, when he was re-admitted as an emergency case three years later due to a psychotic breakdown, he returned to

Fig. 12–7: Heinz

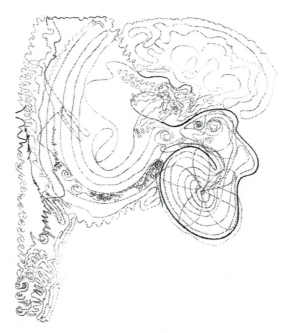

Fig. 12–8: Heinz

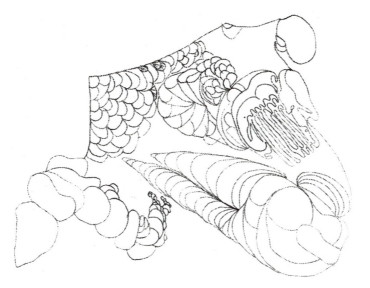

Fig. 12–9: Heinz

drawing. For several hours he drew objects in my room (fig. 12–10, on A4 paper). I understood this to mean that he was able to assure himself of outer reality by drawing it, but at the same he was also gaining a sense of security in linking up to our very first encounters.

Drawing alternately with me enabled Heinz to regulate his contact with me in a way that caused him relatively little anxiety—or perhaps I should say caused him less anxiety—and enabled him thus to allow more of a relationship to develop, even though this opening up was of course extremely limited. This is certainly a phenomenon similar to that observed in Facilitated Communication with autistic people. That too, if properly understood, it is not about the content that is communicated but is essentially about making a relationship easier through relating together to a third element. I have described this elsewhere (Günter, 1990b) in relation to the function of creative art work with psychotic patients. A tangible and visible object in the outside world represents a bridge between therapist and patient, with the therapist's glance not falling directly on the patient but with the two of them looking together at the picture that has been created. In this way the patient can achieve a distancing from the therapist, whom he would otherwise perceive as threatening and intrusive, which he could simply not achieve using language.

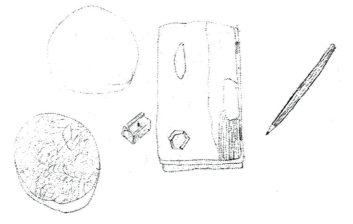

Fig. 12–10: Heinz, Objects from the therapist's room

As a rule we cannot interpret the contents of the pictures in such a context, since the patient's inner world of experience and the relationship are mainly organised through formal aspects, as described in this case vignette. Here classical techniques of a psychoanalytically oriented treatment of psychoses and autistic states are used within the framework of a comprehensive treatment plan. In particular, it is very important to reflect on the induced countertransference. In this case I sensed very clearly how, in the sessions when we were drawing in this variant of the squiggle game, Heinz sought contact and relationship despite his tension and fear, but at the same time made sure I didn't get too close to him. The aggressive moments which seemed to be connected with an inclination to independence on the one hand and a failure of this inclination on the other hand were not apparent to me in the first sessions. They played a major role later, during his treatment as an in-patient and afterwards.

Heinz is now over thirty, seems stable, and has lived for many years in a sheltered home. He works in a workshop for the disabled, and has managed to handle his life quite well on the whole, despite his continuing disability and severe problems with contact. Every now and then we come across each other at some festivity in his earlier residential home and then we exchange a few words, though this tends to be limited to just a few sentences on his part.

CHAPTER THIRTEEN

The rift in the earth and the king's wicked son. The threatening experience of psychosis

Thomas, aged 16

Sixteen-year-old Thomas had been admitted to our clinic on account of a paranoid psychosis. Since spending a two-week holiday overseas staying with an aunt, he had developed a marked obsession with washing based on the fear that he might have infected himself with BSE. Paranoid and compulsive thoughts dominated his thinking and experience. He was in fear of going to Hell: "I'm scared that because of a fault or an omission I will go to Hell," he had said to the doctor who admitted him. He said he received signals to which he had to react, otherwise punishment threatened. Compulsive thoughts, in the form of feelings of guilt and fear of punishment, had started when he had masturbated at around the age of 11. On the ward Thomas developed the notion that he might have infected himself with AIDS through homosexual contacts at the ages of 7 and 14. He was preoccupied with fears that the women on the ward might become pregnant from his sperm. When he masturbated, sperm might be left on the door handles, which would then be touched by the women. His father was described as being under great pressure at work, socially isolated, and depressive and suicidal in phases. The marriage had been difficult for a long time, and the mother was thinking of separating. The boy and his mother largely excluded the father from their relationship, and in particular the father was not allowed to hear of Thomas' problems.

I asked Thomas if he would be willing to take part in a research project and he agreed immediately. We were examining adolescents with psychotic illnesses with regard to the mental images they created, and were making a systematic analysis of psychoanalytical interviews with these young people. In parallel with that we were assessing psychopathological parameters and findings on the family dynamics. At the time of the interview I knew nothing about the family background or the content of his fears and compulsions.

Thomas began the interview, after some hesitation, by drawing a deep rift in the surface of the Earth (fig. 13–1), and talked about how dangerous situations could suddenly arise as a result. In other pictures he introduced a hero and also a racing boat (fig. 13–2, picture 7 in the interview) roaring off over the water in a manic way. In the end it was about the vulnerable sides, those that needed protection. In the further course of the interview he drew a monster with sharp teeth out of my scribble (fig. 13–3, picture 11 in the interview). This was an extra-terrestrial being which either had been found by astronauts on a planet or had surprised them in their ship. It was

Fig. 13–1: Thomas, Rift in the earth

Fig. 13–2: Thomas, Racing boat

caught or killed by the astronauts. Then the danger was gone. From his next squiggle I drew a llama with a rider on its back (fig. 13–4). Presumably I was preoccupied with wondering whether such a monster could not perhaps be tamed. Instead, he preferred a solution he had chosen just before: this was a duckling swimming out alone for the first time, standing on its own feet (fig. 13–5). It was defying the dangers. At this point I commented that on the one hand he wanted to stand courageously on his own two feet and be independent, but on the other hand he was afraid of things which come up suddenly and which he was barely able to cope with. Out of his next squiggle I drew a holster with a pistol, identifying with the phantasies of heroes which were stabilizing his defences (fig. 13–6).

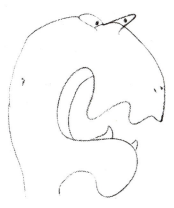

Fig. 13–3: Thomas, Monster with sharp teeth

Fig. 13–4: Thomas, Llama with a rider

Fig. 13–5: Thomas, Duckling

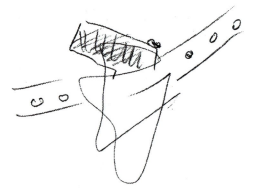

Fig. 13–6: Thomas, Holster with pistol

Out of my next scribble he drew a magician (fig. 13–7). Two friends were trying to recapture a magic stone that he had stolen from them, and were now in danger of being locked up by him. The magic stone gave him too much power, so that he could wreak havoc with it. My interpretation here was that this was obviously a very threatening situation from which escape was likely to be possible only if there were two people and they had help. He nodded. In my next picture (fig. 13–8) I drew a moose antler. He drew a figure in his last picture and explained he had thought of an angel (fig. 13–9), but afterwards it had looked more like someone in a long cape. This was the king's

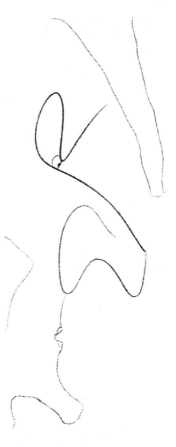

Fig. 13–7: Thomas, Magician

Fig. 13–8: Thomas, Moose antler

Fig. 13–9: Thomas, Angel or the king's wicked son

wicked son. If it was an angel then it would be one who received people into Heaven after their death and gave them a warm-hearted, friendly welcome. The king's son was quite the opposite. He was cold, arrogant and an evil person. He treated his subjects badly, had no sympathy for the people, and would be a bad successor to his father. In conclusion I addressed this: how discrepant these two sides were. Perhaps we needed both, but it was very hard to see these two sides in ourselves. On the next day he asked me who he could talk to about his dreams, saying he didn't understand them.

To sum up, I understood from the course of the interview that he was increasingly emerging from a position of splitting and of omnipotent defence against relationships to formulate the needy and endangered sides of his self. In the course of this, a desire to co-operate with the analyst, who might be able to save him from the evil powers, became apparent. He managed in the end to formulate his inner conflict: that in the process of becoming independent he was finding himself entering into threatening competition with his father, a conflict which did indeed play a central role in his family situation.

This corresponded to the fact that initially the threatening-persecuting parts of his personality were completely projected out in the outside world: in the rifts in the earth, in the monster from outer space. In the course of the interview it became increasingly clear that these could be parts of himself. The wicked magician had "only" stolen the power-conferring, disaster-bearing stone and the friends wanted to have it back. In the end the angel and the king's son characterised relatively clearly the two sides of his self. The king's son was described as cold, arrogant and evil. The angel was warm-hearted and friendly, but this taming of destructive fantasies seemed possible only if libidinous drives were given up: the asexual angel stood at the gate to welcome the dead. The question Thomas posed the next day, asking who he could talk to about his dreams, showed me again that he had begun to grapple with these things as parts of himself and not as threatening him from outside.

Thomas had by no means solved his problems by the end of our interview, but he was now in a better position to consider apparently incompatible inner aspects of his self in his thoughts about the figure. Was he the one who gave people a warm-hearted and friendly welcome or was he the king's evil son treating his subjects—possibly the despised sides of his self—badly? Or was rescue perhaps to be hoped for in the phantasy of an angel-like and thus asexual life beyond the reality of masturbation and sexual drives?

The technique of squiggle interviewing also facilitates making contact even with psychotic patients, who are often extremely uncommunicative in the acute phases of their illness. It is my impression that these patients are happy to have the drawings as a piece of reality to hold on to, and thus find it easier to talk about their inner situation. If their paranoid fears make them feel that a very direct contact with the therapist is intrusive and manipulative, they can distance themselves more easily through the medium of the picture. The presence of a third element between patient and therapist frequently releases the tension in a situation otherwise experienced by the patient as threatening. A second factor is the externalizing and objectifying of the inner worlds through the medium of the picture. Seen in pictures, the threatening inner affects seem to the patients to be easier to handle and to bring under control. This perhaps explains why in my experience many psychotic patients are relatively willing to agree to a squiggle interview of this kind with me. Even adolescents, particularly those who are seriously ill, often have very little objection to doing something as "childish" as playing a squiggle game with me if I explain to them beforehand that I see it as a way of getting to know them a bit better. It is a fact that even with these patients, the squiggle game rapidly opens up unexpected insights into the dynamics of the inner conflicts which unsettle, frighten and disturb them in the course of their psychotic illness. With the help of the squiggle interview it is possible to clarify diagnostic questions and form a picture of the inner situation even of otherwise very taciturn patients. In many cases is it possible, working with the patient, to make such progress in clarifying a point that for that moment a certain relief and structuring can occur. Naturally any lasting stabilization of severe psychotic illnesses in adolescents requires longer-term work involving comprehensive therapeutic approaches at various levels (Du Bois & Günter, 1998).

CHAPTER FOURTEEN

Psychoanalytical access to children under extreme stress: squiggle interviews in research

In the following chapter I am primarily presenting the results of research projects. In a large-scale, long-term project we used the squiggle interview to examine children who had to undergo bone marrow or stem cell transplants (SCT) because of an illness that would otherwise be fatal. The starting point for our research was the examination and treatment of several patients who had developed severe stress reactions after a bone marrow transplant. This raised the question of how other children managed to cope with the stress of treatment, conditioning and isolation. The aims, hypotheses and results of the whole investigation have been described in detail elsewhere (Günter et al, 1997, 1999; Günter, 2003). Here I want to concentrate essentially on describing the inner mechanisms for coping which came to light in the psychoanalytical squiggle interviews with the children.

Why did we use squiggle interviews in our research? There were several reasons, partly to do with methodology and partly determined by pragmatic considerations. First of all, we were anxious to create a space in which these extremely sick children might be able to talk about their problems. The squiggle technique therefore offered us an

"I wish to thank my colleagues Michael Karle, Thomas Klingebiel and Andreas Werning for their work and support. To the children and their families very special thanks are due for agreeing to take part in this despite their difficult situation. Parts of Günter et al, 1997, 1999 and Günter, 2003 have been rewritten to form part of this chapter."

alternative way of making contact with these children (Winnicott, 1971a, p. 3) in a situation where they were willing to take part in and co-operate with the investigation, but would nevertheless not have been willing to talk about their own situation. For here, in this situation of extreme stress, the defences protecting the children from affects of great fear ensured not only that they were inclined to be very quiet and reserved in verbal communication, but also that in the brief initial greeting phase they were mostly quick to tell us that admission to hospital for the transplant was no great problem for them. It would all go well, most of the children indicated to us in one way or another, and anyway they didn't want to talk any further about it. By contrast, the children were easily won over to the idea of a squiggle interview, and then usually let themselves get deeply involved.

In terms of method, we were confronted with what Cronbach (1970) described as the bandwidth-fidelity dilemma. The more we limit the personality traits we collect, the more reliable the results we can achieve as a rule (and perhaps the more valid according to the classical criteria of psychological testing). The more comprehensive and true to life an examination of the whole situation is (for example using psychoanalytical interviews or projective tests), the more problematic it is to determine its reliability and validity in the classical sense. To put it simply, I always have the choice between an experimental situation, which can register a specific point very reliably but may say very little about the child's real situation, and a more clinically-oriented examination, which captures the child in all the complexity of his or her reactions but, it must be said, produces results which have a clear subjective tinge. For this reason we decided to proceed on two tracks in our study of bone marrow and stem cell transplants. On the one hand we used self-assessment scales and similar procedures whose objectivity, reliability and validity had been tested according to classical criteria; and on the other hand we used projective procedures and a squiggle interview. The squiggle interviews gave us a comprehensive picture of the child's emotional situation, but were of course, particularly in those parts which allowed very deep insights into the child's inner situation, coloured by the always subjective relationship between the child and myself.

At times I was seen by the child as a "subjective object" (Winnicott, 1971a; Bürgin, 1992). This means that the child projected his or her conflicts onto me and onto the situation, which was, of course, precisely what was intended for the diagnostic process. One example of this type of projection might be the picture described in Chapter 1 (fig. 1–1) from the squiggle interview with eight-year-old Oliver, who had undergone a transplant two weeks earlier for aplastic anaemia. Projective mechanisms dominated: it was the interviewer whose appearance had changed, not the patient himself. These projective mechanisms meant that the interviewer was himself powerfully drawn into the psychic process and, in comparison with a verbally-based psychotherapeutic conversation, had little protection from the setting (Bürgin, 1978, 1992). Deep identifications with the patient and equally rapid distancing were just as necessary as keeping control over our own projections and other defence manoeuvres; the particular problems of these in the treatment of patients with fatal illnesses were described in detail by Eissler (1970). In using this technique when treating children in such life-threatening situations, we had to be particularly conscious of the fact that there was always a risk of circumventing the young patient's defences. For this reason, Winnicott's strongly expressed admonition that the child should always have the opportunity to reject or correct interpretations made by the interviewer is of particular importance here.

Taking these factors into consideration, the psychoanalytical squiggle interview was an essential tool for describing the patients' emotional situation, and a valuable complement on the one hand to the questionnaires, which essentially showed their conscious self-perception and presentation of self to others, and on the other hand to the projective tests, which registered their more unconscious processes. In particular, the interviews very quickly produced a depiction of quite specific individual conflict dynamics. This was to be seen as the result of existing personality and dynamics as influenced by the current acute situation. Bürgin (1978) has already pointed to the fruitfulness of such an approach in the examination of children with cancer.

Severe, life-threatening illnesses in childhood of course place extreme stress not only on the children affected but also on their entire family. The possible death of the child is often a spectre haunting them over years, even if what is uppermost in the child's conscious mind, particularly in the critical phases, is summed up by Pausanias in Hölderlin's Der Tod des Empedocles [The Death of Empedocles]: "Death, I know him little. For seldom did I think of him." The denial of death in conscious thought is an ever-present experience in the treatment of children with life-threatening diseases. This psychosocial adaptation, which in most cases is extraordinarily efficient and often astonishingly successful, is nevertheless accompanied by an intense inner grappling with life and death, deep fear, despair, helplessness and feelings of narcissistic injury and fury (Bürgin, 1978; Günter, 2003). This struggle can often barely be discerned from the outside, at least as long as everything is going reasonably well; the extent of the stress only becomes apparent on more intensive examination of the preconscious and unconscious processes. At times there will be explosive stress reactions and severe disturbance of adaptation: at moments when an anticipated turn for the better does not occur, or there is a setback, or some infection that other children would consider banal unleashes a wave of preconscious fears that this is a relapse.

To make the situation in which these children find themselves a bit easier to follow, let me give a rough outline of the procedure involved in a bone marrow or stem cell transplant. Stem cell transplantation has become a standard clinical method for the treatment of malign illnesses. It is also used as a therapy (in many cases still an experimental one) for other illnesses, particularly for genetic defects. In Germany at the present time, more than 300 children receive a bone marrow transplant each year. After the indication is given, the children undergo comprehensive diagnostic examinations. As a rule, repeated stays in hospital for diagnostic and therapeutic purposes are part of the child's previous experience. About two weeks after the fresh diagnosis, the children are admitted to the SCT ward for their transplant. The first step is called conditioning: this is the removal of the remaining bone marrow through whole-body radiotherapy and/or large doses of cytostatic drugs. About six days after admission to the SCT ward, the transplant is carried out in the form of an intravenous infusion of bone marrow or stem cells via a Hickman catheter. The children spend this time and about another three weeks in a single room and are treated under isolation conditions in the laminar air flow unit.

The laminar air flow unit is actually a room built within a room to create a germ-free environment. With considerable noise from the ventilation unit, a laminar air flow (a turbulence-free outward air flow) is generated in order to stir up as little dust as possible. (I am describing the situation as it was when we carried out the research; in the meantime a new paediatric clinic has been built in Tübingen, including a new SCT ward with significantly improved accommodation.) Water is filtered of germs; toys are disinfected or packed in boxes, shrink-wrapped and given a dose of gamma radiation. The TV set is outside the room and the remote control is also shrink-wrapped after gamma-radiation. The door is open and provisioning is from outside. The monitoring, infusion and other equipment is also outside.

Parents and, if necessary, medical staff can enter the room wearing a surgical mask, after changing their clothes and undergoing disinfection. The children are as a rule severely affected physically by the conditioning. In particular, we can mention problems with the mucous membranes, pain, diarrhoea etc; their general physical condition is greatly weakened. Subjectively, many children are very much preoccupied with the total loss of their hair. There can be many complications: graft-versus-host reaction, i.e. an immune attack by the transplanted marrow on the child's body, is common and can take on life-threatening proportions depending on which organ systems are affected. Infections with rapid development of sepsis are a problem, but as a rule can be brought under control. Systemic mycosis can be a particular problem. As soon as a sufficiently high leukocyte count is reached, about three weeks after the transplant (about four weeks after admission to the isolation room) at the earliest, the children can be moved to an open room on the same ward. From there, depending on how things go, they are discharged after another few days, and can go home. However, at home they still have to wear a surgical mask over their mouth for another 100 days or so when they are with people outside the family.

The following description is of two connected prospective longitudinal studies which we carried out between 1994 and 2000 to record children's emotional situation and coping strategies. The first examination (t1) was carried out two weeks before admission for SCT and the second (t2) two weeks after transplant (average 14.3 ± 2.3 days), while the children were still being treated in a single room under isolation conditions (Günter et al, 1997, 1999). The third examination (t3) was carried out two and a half years after the transplant (average 2.61 ± 0.67 years) (Günter, 2003), as a rule at the child's home. The standardized tools mentioned earlier essentially registered the child's conscious experience with regard to depression, stress caused by anxiety, and sense of their own body image, and gave neuroticism and extroversion scores. Alongside these results we placed the psychoanalytical interview using the squiggle technique and the projective tests, which focused more on the preconscious and unconscious sides of the child's inner life. With this mixed approach to the research we were able to document and contrast various levels of the child's psychical organisation and ways of experiencing. It was also important to limit the age group to 8–12-year-olds, since we could assume that different coping mechanisms would be used by different age groups. Of the 30 patients we examined, 18 were still alive after two and a half years, and 15 of those took part in the follow-up study. Of these 15 patients, one had a relapse, and for another the possibility of relapse could not be excluded with certainty. All the others were in relatively good or very good health; however, some suffered impairments resulting from the treatment: slower growth, contractures, slight graft-versus-host illnesses, and the threat of sterility.

In our examination before and during the transplant, most of the children showed in their behaviour a near-perfect realistic accommodation to the demands of the treatment, accompanied by a mild depressive reaction, avoidance of the theme and slight regressive tendencies. In the self-assessment questionnaire, this adaptation resulted in an "over-normalisation" of the scores for anxiety, depression, neuroticism and extroversion, with a relatively undifferentiated sense of their own body. In a significant deviation from the values in the normal population, the children stated that they had no fear, they were not depressive, and they were extroverted and outgoing, that is to say they were definitely not suffering from stress. This "over-normalisation" was even more marked at the time of the second examination, which was when they were being treated in a single room in isolation conditions. This result became highly significant when the individual dimensions measured were aggregated. We understood this, exactly in the sense of the Hölderlin quotation, as the expression of a successful strategy of denial in the conscious levels of experience. In particular, in contrast to what one might naively have expected, the differentiated perception of their bodies was strongly repressed as part of this coping strategy.

The results of the Rorschach test and the squiggle interviews, which represented the more unconscious levels of emotional organisation, showed a different aspect. In these deeper layers, the children occupied themselves intensely with feelings and phantasies relating to their life-threatening illness and its treatment (cf. the squiggle interviews with Klaus and Elke described in Chapters 10 and 11). This preoccupation was intensified during the time they spent in hospital compared to the time before admission. The interviews afforded varied insights into the organisation of defences and the children's impressive coping strategies. The frequent mention—in comparison to a normal sample—of poison and of oral-aggressive moments (Table 14–1, columns Sq1 and Sq2) seemed relatively specific, and this could also be seen in the squiggle interviews conducted by Bürgin with cancer patients (1978). Depending on the degree and the context, these results pointed to an intense unconscious occupation with existential fear at the oral-aggressive level, which we normally find to this extent only in patients with severe deficits in affect and ego organisation. In terms of themes, they focused above all on poisonous animals, some of which were armed with spikes or teeth. In addition, the patients very often drew pictures showing varying degrees of manifest deep-seated paranoid fears of being eaten, devoured and robbed of their identity (Table 14–2, columns Sq1 and Sq 2). When we considered how threatening their situation was, how overwhelmed they felt, how much life-threatening poison they had to consume in the form of cytostatic and other drugs, and the extent to which archaic aggressive impulses were thereby activated, then these largely unconscious fears were very understandable. For example, 13-year-old Jakob was suffering from adrenoleucodystrophy, an X-linked recessive disorder affecting the metabolism of fatty acids which, if untreated, leads to degeneration of the brain and finally to death. First of all he drew a squid which he said was very dangerous. After that he drew a precise and completely individual depiction of his existentially threatening situation: an apple with "core twister-outer" (fig. 14–1). The picture showed how the core was being removed from the apple with the help of an instrument. This was impressive as a drastic picture of Jakob's situation, in which his core, the bone marrow, was in effect being twisted out by the conditioning. At a psychic level this brought up the existential question of identity. In the following picture he turned the squiggle into a butcher's hook, which in this context could only be understood as continuing the depiction of these archaic fears threatening him in undifferentiated form.

What was noticeable was that such phantasies were less frequently made the subject of pictures in the second squiggle interview (7 falling to 3 for poison and 20 falling to 9 for oral persecution fears).

Table 14–1: The theme of poison in the squiggle interviews

Patient no.	Squiggle interview 1 (2 weeks before admission)	Sq1	Squiggle interview 2 (2 weeks after transplant)	Sq2	Squiggle interview 3 (2½ years after transplant)	Sq3
1					✠	
2						
3						
4						
5	1;4 poisonous snake	1				
6						
7						
8					✠	
9					3;5 fly agaric toadstool ✠	1
10	1;5 tarantulas	1	2;8 stinging bees	1		
11	**1;1** poison-spitting snake 1;5 ray, poisonous sting 1;15 poison-squirting octopus	3				
12	1;25 cobra	1	2;7 poisonous snake	1		
13	1;9 poisonous mushroom	1	2;8 **non-**poisonous snake	1		
14					third interview refused ✠	
15						
Total		7		3		1

Sq1 = Squiggle Interview 1 (two weeks before admission); Sq 2 = Squiggle Interview 2 (two weeks after transplant, still in single room under isolation conditions); Sq3 = Squiggle Interview 3 (2½ years after transplant). The number in bold refers to the squiggle interview, the number after the semicolon refers to the number of the picture in the interview.
✠ means the child did not survive to a third interview.

Table 14–2: The theme of oral aggression in squiggle interviews

Patient no.	Oral aggression			Sq1	Sq2	Sq3
	severe	moderate	slight			
1			**1**; 16 tomcat eats mouse	1		✠
2		**1**,4 snake eats rabbit without chewing		1		
3	**3**;7 man-eating dinosaur		**1**;12 wolf	1		
4			**1**;19 hungry snake **2**;11 teeth of the monster	1	1	1
5		**2**;11 greedy face			1	
6			(**2**;9 caterpillar)		(1)	
7	**1**;7 vampire **1**;9 monster with teeth			2		
8		**1**;19 killer whale	**1**;1 snake with tongue **1**;5 dinosaur with tongue (**3**;1 meat on bone)	1		✠
9	**2**;7 man-eating snake	**2**;9 extra-terrestrial being eating **2**;11 shark		2	3	(1)
10	**1**;1 gaping mouth **1**;2 huge shark **1**;5 witch, natives eat tarantulas			3		✠
11	**1**;17 octopus, sperm whale **2**;11 octopus			1	1	
12		**2**;6 hypnotising snake from *The Jungle Book*			1	re-fused
13	**1**;15 apple, core removed **1**;17 butcher's hook	**1**;13 octopus	**1**;7 **vegetarian dinosaur**	4		
14	**1**;13 butcher's hook	**1**;19 octopus **1**; 21 bait on angler's hook		3		✠
15			**2**;11 shark		1	
Total				**20**	**9**	**2**

Sq1 = Squiggle Interview 1 (two weeks before admission); Sq 2 = Squiggle Interview 2 (two weeks after transplant, still in single room under isolation conditions); Sq3 = Squiggle Interview 3 (2½ years after transplant). The number in bold refers to the squiggle interview, the number after the semicolon refers to the number of the picture in the interview. ✠ means the child did not survive to a third interview.

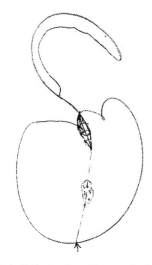

Fig. 14–1: Jakob (13), Apple with core "twister-outer" (sic)

These results underlined the children's perceptible relief from destructive and threatening affects of fear after the transplant had been carried out and they were being treated under isolation conditions in a single room. In order to overcome their fear, the children now increasingly took refuge in a regressive need for dependence, which seemed more socially acceptable in the hospital context. These appeared sometimes as clear childish regressive wishes, and sometimes also as wishes for loving care at an oral level. Clinically this became apparent in how much they leaned on their parents, which at times extended to exercising an infant-like tyranny over them. Often a close emotional bond with the nurses caring for them could also be observed. Thirteen days after his stem-cell transplant, Jakob had his second interview with me, which took place in the isolation room. Among other things, he drew a mole poking its head out of a hole with a piece of egg-shell on its head, as if it were a chick just hatching out of its egg (fig. 14–2). I took this to be an emotional expression of his present situation and I found it very moving. It seemed helpful that he could fall back on regressive tendencies to ward off primitive persecution fears. In the course of the conversation he drew a deck chair and talked about how nice it would be to go on holiday. In the last picture he continued the theme by drawing a playground with play equipment and a paddling pool

Fig. 14–2: Jakob (13), Mole with egg shell

for young children. This too appeared to be a regressive tendency which was completely appropriate for the situation. Such mild regressive developments were to be regarded clinically as favourable defence mechanisms.

Phantasies of fleeing also played a major role in maintaining psychical balance (cf. Table 14–3). Nearly all our patients depicted such phantasies in the squiggle interviews. The phantasies themselves were astonishingly varied and individual. They often had a clear biographical reference and also a close connection to the children's fundamental psychodynamics. In our analysis of the interviews, it struck us that in the second interview all the patients who had shown pronounced stress reactions produced either no manifest phantasy of fleeing or only a "negative" one, by which I mean that their pictures depicted phantasies in which flight was attempted but prevented. There can be little doubt about the enormous importance of such phantasies of fleeing for the regulation of affects, for the ability to adapt to this stressful situation and for the ability to co-operate; though what causal relationship there was between phantasies of fleeing and stress reactions remains an open question. Did the lack of a hopeful perspective, as expressed in the lack of phantasies of fleeing, cause a severe stress reaction, or was the severe stress reaction, generally connected with a severe depressive restriction, responsible for the child's inability to produce phantasies of fleeing? Whatever the case, this was one of the results that struck me as important in terms of how to deal with these patients clinically and in terms of creating a "facilitating environment".

Table 14-3: Manifest phantasies of fleeing in squiggle interviews

Patient no.	Sq1	Theme	Sq2	Theme	Stress reaction
1	3	I'm going to be given a little rabbit at home when I've recovered	9 13	Flying a kite Call of the mountains, home country	
2	10	Idea: a person hiding in a cave in wartime	10	There is a way out **but you can easily get lost**	x
3	11	**Bear on a chain so it can't escape and frighten people**	3	Flying bird	
4	17	Balloon	15 17	Dog, he wants to see his dog again Snail in its shell	
5	3 7 9	Viking ship Aeroplane towing something Dragon flying away	3 5	Flying dragon Slightly crumpled balloon	
6	-		-		x
7	17	Castle with emergency staircase	1 6	Balloon with a person Rising balloon	
8	(4) 19 20	Doesn't look when drawing for fear of falling down dead **Free Willy, caught** Pun: Go	+	In conversation: thinks of home	

9	7	Road seen from above, with different paths leading off it	Picnic and cave to sleep in, sheltering from rain	11	
	11	Looking through telescope at stars			
	13	Walking out of rain into sunshine			
10	9	Enchanting Jenny	**Hour-glass** **Boy, tied up** Idea: riding away on his bike	5 6 7	x
11	11	Journey with first aid kit and emergency equipment		–	x
	13	Earthworm can flee in either direction			
12	5	Ostrich with its head in the sand		–	x
	19	Idea: her bird has flown away			
13	3, 12	Cave in his home country, Italy	Deck chair Playground for children	10 12	
14	9, 12, 15, 17	Race track, motorway, bicycle, car	refused		
15		Idea: he is flying off astride my doll's house	Flying squirrel Shark leaping upwards Pointed drill boring a tunnel	6 11 15	

The themes in which the motif of fleeing is perhaps questionable are printed in bold. The numbers refer to the pictures in the interview.

Another important defence mechanism was the narcissistic phantasies which manifested themselves in many areas. In general, we noted that narcissistic and manic defence tendencies played a greater role in the first interviews, while in the second their place was taken by the regressive tendencies mentioned above, and they were sometimes also replaced by a more open tackling of depressive factors. Narcissistic attempts to cope could be observed on the one hand in terms of performance, in an emphasis on ability to perform, and sometimes also in a projection of deficits onto the interviewer. On the other hand, manic defence tendencies were found in the way the whole experience of illness was depicted as a party, as pleasure, or in Balint's sense (1959) as a thrill, particularly when deeply rooted fears came to the surface. For boys in particular, phallic-narcissistic defence tendencies were also important. Power, strength, speed etc. were very frequent themes.

However, what was absolutely central as a rule was how narcissistic defence manoeuvres were connected with warding off the experience of feeling defective. This area was made a theme in both first and second squiggle interviews by the majority of the patients. Often this experience of feeling defective was closely connected to the depiction of bodily deficits. In both interviews, more than half the patients referred directly to bodily deficits in their drawings. In part these were defects that had emerged as a result of their illness and its treatment. In particular, loss of hair and damage to the mucous membranes after conditioning or after earlier chemotherapy were often unconsciously but unmistakably depicted. In some cases, restrictions of bodily functions independent of the illness were addressed in the pictures.

Beyond these themes, there were repeated clear signs of a loss of differentiation in the body scheme and a loss of clear outline, which might be regarded as being very closely connected to a fundamental loss of confidence in ego identity (Günter, 1995). The theme of bodily defect, largely denied in conscious conversation, and the theme of threat to identity was touched on by practically all the patients through pictures of specifically identified deformations of human or animal bodies. Often a proximity to phantasies of death was also noticeable. The squiggle technique was a particularly appropriate medium in which to depict such body-related phantasies. This was already apparent in Winnicott's squiggles (Winnicott, 1971a), though he himself made no explicit reference to it, and to my knowledge there is no literature on this subject.

Very closely connected to this theme was the depiction of sexual phantasies. It was striking that all four girls in the study, regardless of their age, were intensely occupied with sexual phantasies. It seemed that for all four girls, the problem of sterility, which was expected to result from the conditioning, played an important part in the squiggle interview, whereas it did not crop up in the interviews with the boys. Baby-phantasies and oedipal phantasies, the latter presumably against the background of an oedipal situation not satisfactorily resolved before the illness, played a large part in the first squiggle interview, and continued with three of the four girls in the second. It is worth noting that there were clear, though certainly not unexpected differences here. Whereas all the girls were intensely concerned with the narcissistic injury as it concerned their sexuality, and as a rule compensated with a narcissistic cathexis of the body (as is also specified for them culturally in the female role), for the boys, the narcissistic injury through bodily defect was not nearly as often or as closely connected with sexuality, and was warded off with a narcissistic cathexis of outward phallic attributes such as cars etc. rather than of the body. This difference could not be explained simply in terms of age difference. The boys (average age 10.2) were nearly a year older than the girls (average age 9.3), so that the stage of psycho-sexual development—if we take into account the slightly earlier development of girls at this age—must have been the same.

I carried out a further examination of the children who were still alive after two and a half years. Both the children and their parents, almost without exception, reported at that time that social re-integration had gone well. The patients had many friends. Nearly all the children were described as being relatively good and fitting in well. Despite the long spells in hospital, school results were good. The way they had dealt emotionally with the illness and the transplant was described as inconspicuous. There was just one girl who had shown some symptoms of post-traumatic stress disorder for a short time after her discharge. All the children said that they occasionally remembered their illness but tried to think about it as little as possible. Outwardly, therefore, after two and a half years their psychosocial adaptation was outstanding.

Accordingly, we had expected the results obtained from the questionnaire to have normalised. But to our surprise, even two and half years after the stem cell transplant, the children still described themselves, in a way that deviated significantly from the norm for their age, as not depressive, not afraid, very outgoing and extro-verted, and they still had extremely low values for their differentia-tion of body image. This corresponded largely to the scores which had been registered at the time of maximum stress before the transplant, and in some areas the "positive" deviation from the norm was even more accentuated. What we saw was a kind of continuing "over-normalisation" in central areas of the consciously accessible experience of self. In the Rorschach test, we found stronger tendencies to concern themselves with inner processes, with less externalised processing and a more pronounced facing up to reality. There were also indications that the permanent limitations resulting from the illness were having a stronger adverse effect.

We had to assume on the basis of these results that although outward psychosocial adaptation was very good, intense inner coping processes were continuing, though it became clear that the stress caused by threatening and destructive phantasies had further reduced (Table 14–1; Table 14–2, column Sq3). Building on these findings, the psychoanalytical squiggle interviews could give us information on the themes which were still of central importance to the children, which weighed on them, and which they overcame at the cost of considerable psychical effort even two and half years after the transplant:

1. Problems with their own sexuality were found in the children almost without exception. In particular, the threat of sterility played a large part in their inner lives. The associated fears and phantasies of inferiority, insufficient potency and attractiveness were not overcome.
2. The sensitivity and vulnerability of their body appeared in many variations. Preoccupation with this took the place of primitive phantasies of aggressive threat.
3. Fears of death, fear of a relapse, and phantasies of being alone and abandoned were found in many of the children. In connection with this, their perspectives of the future were often dimmed. These fears were reactivated in particular

during other intermittently occurring illnesses, and the children's behaviour remained hard to understand without knowledge of this inner connection.

4. In order to stabilize themselves, alongside a mainly anxious and cautious basic attitude with a high level of adaptation and ability to achieve, the children used various unconscious strategies in parallel: infantile and regressive behaviour and psychical prematurity, narcissistic presentation of self and accentuation of their own strength, and extensive time spent doing things on their own.

In summary, we could say that the children achieved their astonishing adaptation, both at the time of the transplant and two and half years later, by dealing with the experience on at least two levels. The outward and visible normalisation was achieved at the level accessible to conscious thought by maintaining strategies of denial towards affects of depression and fear. This made it easier for the children to return to normality despite having faced existential threat. On a more unconscious level of psychic organisation, they were still grappling with central questions of life and with fears which they had not fully been able to overcome and which still represented a source of stress. In particular, fears regarding sexual development, the experience of bodily deficits and of their own vulnerability, but also buried feelings of anger over their fate played a great role and strained their ability to regulate their narcissism. In normal life these children still could not talk about these problems, because a conscious discussion of them would have jeopardised the psychosocial adaptation which was so important. Two years and three months after his transplant, 13-year-old Florian summed up this dilemma precisely in a picture in his squiggle interview (fig. 14–3): a dinosaur with a cap and goatee beard, and he was jolly, wearing a costume. On my asking him about it, Florian added that it was a mixture of dangerous and jolly because of the dangerous teeth. I have since heard that Florian suffered a relapse of his neuroblastoma and died.

At the beginning of this chapter I quoted Pausanias' line "Death, I know him little . . ." without giving Empedocles' answer, which was: "To be alone and without gods is death." For some, the gods are what Freud called "the Other of the heavenly powers", namely

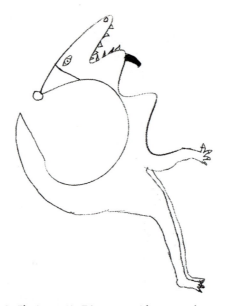

Fig. 14–3: Florian (13), Dinosaur with cap and goatee beard,
he is jolly and wearing a costume. Because of his dangerous teeth he's a
mixture of dangerous and jolly.

the eternal Eros, the loving tie to parents, brothers and sisters. For some it is religion which, together with the family, offers consolation and support. But for some it is also the phantasy of fleeing, of a *deus ex machina* making all end well, perhaps in the form of a phantasy journey to faraway lands. Or it lies in changing one's own appearance, as with Wiebke, now 12, who dyed her thinning hair electric green after chemotherapy. She tried through a narcissistic cathexis of her endangered body to overcome her grief over permanent sterility and her fears of insufficiency as a woman. We as therapists can only try to be open to the phantasies of our patients and to take up gently and carefully what in that particular situation they are able to say and seems right to them. My work with these children has convinced me that the "intermediate realm of phantasy" (Freud 1916/17) not only has the power to capture destructive threat in images but also offers relief and consolation, and makes reality seem worth living.

Alongside the qualitative and partial quantitative analysis of the interviews described here on the basis of detailed records or transcripts, squiggle interviews can also be quantified with the help of an external rating. We achieved quite a good correlation from two independent raters in the evaluation of "global psychic level of function" (correlation coefficient $r = 0.70$), "emotional openness and ability to relate" ($r = 0.73$) and "clarity in dealing with the situation emotionally" ($r = 0.75$), and slightly less for fear ($r = 0.45$), depression ($r = 0.61$) and aggression ($r = 0.73$). Since then, in a study of adolescents with first-time psychotic illness, we have tried to develop a rating manual tailored to specific questions. The interview situation was slightly altered in that I asked the adolescents to tell me a short story around each squiggle-picture. The stories can be analysed individually according to the manual, and corresponding points can be added together over and above the stories and combined in larger scales, so that one set of squiggle-pictures and the stories accompanying them can be compared to those of other adolescents. Of course these more objective evaluation strategies only cover a small part of the wealth of material contained in the squiggle interviews which can be put to good clinical use. To that extent, they are not intended as a means of placing the clinical use of the squiggle game on an objective basis, so to speak. Winnicott already warned against doing that, and was right to do so (1968). Nevertheless, the richness of the material and its inner structure, which can be divided easily into separate sections following the pictures, may also open up new ways of understanding a more objective evaluation, and new opportunities for viewing parts of the clinical material from different angles. The fact that the squiggle game is also accepted by very sick children, the chance it offers to gain psychic material indirectly, and the fact that the drawings and the incidental notes on them can be remarkably helpful in the systematic documentation and evaluation of the interviews all make these conversations an extraordinarily exciting clinical research tool, even if a relatively large outlay of time and energy is required to collect the material and to develop appropriate evaluation methods.

REFERENCES

Abram, J. (1996). *The Language of Winnicott: A Dictionary of Winnicott's Use of Words*. London: Karnac.

Argelander, H. (1970). *Das erste interview in der Psychotherapie*. Darmstadt: Wissenschaftliche Buchgesellschaft (quoted here according to the 6th unrevised edition, Darmstadt, Primus 1999).

Arnheim, Rudolf (1954). *Art and Visual Perception*. University of California Press.

Arnheim, Rudolf (1982). Gestaltpsychologie und künstlerische Form. In: Dieter Henrich & Wolfgang Iser (Eds.), *Theorien der Kunst* (pp. 132–147). Frankfurt/M: Suhrkamp.

Balint, M. (1959). *Thrills and Regressions*. London: Hogarth.

Baxandall, M. (1985). *Patterns of Intention*. Yale University Press.

Berger, L.R. (1980). The Winnicott squiggle game: a vehicle for communicating with the school-aged child. *Pediatrics, 66*: 921–924.

Bion, W.R. (1962). *Learning from Experience*. London: Heinemann.

Brafman, A.H. (1997). Winnicott's therapeutic consultations revisited. *International Journal of Psycho-Analysis 78*: 773–787.

Branik, Emil (2001). Zum Stellenwert der Psychoanalyse in der stationären Kinder- und Jugendpsychiatrie. *Kinderanalyse 9*: 1–21.

Branik, Emil (2002). Inszenierungen unter Einsatz des Körpers in der Psychotherapie von Jugendlichen. *Kinderanalyse 10*: 40–61.

Bürgin, D. (1978). *Das Kind, die lebensbedrohende Krankheit und der Tod*. Bern, Stuttgart, Wien: Huber.

Bürgin, D. (1992). Zur Indikation psychoanalytischer Psychotherapie bei Kindern und Jugendlichen. *Kinderanalyse 1*: 22–45.

Claman, L. (1980). The squiggle-drawing game in child psychotherapy. *American Journal of Psychotherapy 34*: 414–425.

Cronbach, L. (1970). *Essentials of Psychological Testing*. New York: Harper.

Di Gallo, A. (2000). Die Zeichnung als Brücke beim Erstkontakt mit dem krebskranken Kind. *Kinderanalyse 8*: 376–395.

Eissler, K.R. (1970). *The Psychiatrist and the Dying Patient*. International Universities Press.

Erikson, E.H. (1956). The Problem of Ego Identity. *Psychological Issues I*: 101–164.

Farhi, N. (2001). Psychotherapy and the Squiggle Game: A Sophisticated Game of Hide-and-Seek. In: M. Bertolini, A. Giannakoulas, M. Hernandez, *Squiggles and Spaces. Revisiting the Work of D.W. Winnicott, Vol. 2* (pp. 65–75). London: Whurr.

Freud, A. (1927). The methods of Child Analysis. In: *Writings, 1* (pp. 19–35). New York: IUP.

Freud, S. (1911b). Formulations on the two principles of mental functioning. *SE 12*: 218–226.

Freud, S. (1916/17). Introductory Lectures on Psycho-analysis. *SE 15/16*.

Freud, S. (1920g). Beyond the Pleasure Principle. *SE 18*.

Gombrich, Ernst H. (1960). *Art and Illusion* (quoted according to the 5th edition, 5th impression 1987, p. 159). Oxford: Phaidon Press.

Günter, M. (1989). *Gestaltungstherapie. Zur Geschichte der Mal-Ateliers in Psychiatrischen Kliniken*. Bern, Stuttgart, Toronto: Huber.

Günter, M. (1990a). Gestaltungstherapie in der Psychiatrischen Klinik: Eine historische Analyse der Entstehung von Malateliers. *Psychiatrische Praxis, 17*: 163–171.

Günter, M. (1990b). Malen im therapeutischen Prozess mit psychotischen Jugendlichen: Ein Mittel zur Regulierung von Nähe und Distanz. In: R. Lempp (Ed.), *Die Therapie im Jugendalter* (pp. 60–70). Bern, Stuttgart, Toronto: Huber.

Günter, M. (1993). Zu den kunsttheoretischen Grundlagen heutiger gestaltungstherapeutischer Praxis. *Zeitschrift für Kunstgeschichte, 57*: 278–288.

Günter, M. (1995). "Ich bin ich" – Das Bild des eigenen Körpers als Beziehungsangebot: Affirmation der Identität angesichts ihrer Bedrohung. *Kinderanalyse, 4*: 201–219.

Günter, M., Werning, A., Karle, M., & Klingebiel, T. (1997). Abwehrprozesse als Adaptationsleistung: Ein psychoanalytischer Zugang zu Kindern unter Knochenmarktransplantation im Life Island. *Kinderanalyse, 5*: 124–152.

Günter, M. & Du Bois, R. (1998). The Adolescent Psychotic and the Context of Residential Treatment. In: J. Pestalozzi, S. Frisch, R.D. Hinshelwood,

& D. Houzel (Eds.), *Psychoanalytic Psychotherapy in Institutional Settings* (pp. 141–160). London: Karnac.

Günter, M., Karle, M., Werning, A. & Klingebiel, Th. (1999). Emotional adaptation of children undergoing bone marrow transplantation. *Canadian Journal of Psychiatry*, 44: 77–81.

Günter, M. (2000). Art Therapy as an Intervention to Stabilize the Defenses of Children Undergoing Bone Marrow Transplantation. *The Arts in Psychotherapy*, 27: 3–14.

Günter, M. (2002). Agieren, Deuten und Durcharbeiten. Die Wechselwirkung von Therapie und Pädagogik auf einer Schulkinderstation. *Kinderanalyse*, 10: 161–176.

Günter, M. (2003). Extrembelastung unter Isolationsbehandlung bei Stammzelltransplantation. Realgefahr und Fantasiebewältigung. In: G. Klosinski (Ed.), *Grenz- und Extremerfahrungen im interdisziplinären Dialog* (pp. 156–174). Tübingen: Attempto.

Hoffman, Donald D. (1998). *Visual Intelligence: How we create what we see.* New York.

Klein, M. (1932). *The Psycho-analysis of Children.* London: Hogarth.

Klein, M. (1946). Notes on some schizoid mechanisms. *International Journal of Psychoanalysis*, 27: 99–110.

Klein, M. (1957). *Envy and Gratitude: A Study of Unconscious Forces.* New York: Basic Books.

Kris, E. (1936). Bemerkungen zur Bildnerei der Geisteskranken. *Imago*, 22: 339–370.

Kris, E. (1952). *Psychoanalytic Explorations in Art.* New York: International Universities Press.

Leonardo da Vinci. *The Notebooks.*

Loch, W. (2006). *The Art of Interpretation.* London: IPA; Tübingen: Edition diskord.

Winnicott, D.W. (1954). Metapsychological and Clinical Aspects of Regression within the Psycho-Analytical Set-Up. *International Journal of Psychoanalysis*, 36: 16.

Winnicott, D.W. (1960). The Theory of the Parent-Infant Relationship. *International Journal of Psycho-Analysis*, 41: 585–595.

Winnicott, D.W. (1968). The Squiggle Game. In: C. Winnicott, R. Shepherd & M. Davis, *Psycho-Analytic Explorations* (pp. 299–317). London: Karnac, 1989.

Winnicott, D.W. (1971a). *Therapeutic Consultations in Child Psychiatry.* London: Hogarth (Karnac, 1996).

Winnicott, D.W. (1971b). *Playing and Reality.* London: Tavistock

Winnicott, D.W. (1984). *Deprivation and Delinquency.* London: Tavistock.

LIST OF ILLUSTRATIONS

INDEX

Page references in italics indicate illustrations